AN INTRODUCTION TO
SECOND TEMPLE JUDAISM

AN INTRODUCTION TO SECOND TEMPLE JUDAISM

History and Religion of the Jews in the
Time of Nehemiah, the Maccabees,
Hillel and Jesus

LESTER L. GRABBE

t&t clark

Published by T&T Clark International
A Continuum Imprint
The Tower Building, 11 York Road, London SE1 7NX
80 Maiden Lane, Suite 704, New York, NY 10038

www.continuumbooks.com

British Library Cataloguing-in-Publication Data
A catalogue record for this book is available from the British Library

ISBN: 978-0-567-05161-5 (Hardback)
       978-0-567-55248-8 (Paperback)

Typeset by Newgen Imaging Systems Pvt Ltd, Chennai, India
Printed and bound in Great Britain by
CPI Antony Rowe Ltd, Chippenham, Wiltshire

To my students of early Judaism

CONTENTS

3 REVOLUTIONARY JUDAISM: THE POLITICAL AND 'MESSIANIC' CURRENT

4 ESCHATOLOGICAL JUDAISM: THE APOCALYPTIC CURRENT

PREFACE

This book is an introduction to Judaism of the Second Temple period. That is, it covers the time beginning in the Persian period and ending with the fall of the temple (539 BCE–70 CE), though I find it helpful to go as late as the Bar Kokhba revolt (132–35 CE). I have already given a detailed history of the Judaism of the period in *Judaism from Cyrus to Hadrian* (1992) and the four-volume work, *History of the Jews and Judaism in the Second Temple Period* (vol. 1 [2004], vol. 2 [2008], and vols 3–4 [in preparation]), so what I am doing in this much briefer study is to try to introduce the beginner – the student, the educated lay person, the non-specialist – to the subject. As the title of the present book indicates, I focus on the first century BCE and CE. (It is the convention now among scholars of early Judaism to use the abbreviations CE and BCE when giving dates. They stand for 'Common Era' [CE] and 'Before the Common Era' [BCE], being equivalent to AD and BC.) However, I do not limit myself to those two centuries since a complete understanding of them requires a general knowledge of the preceding several centuries.

Chapter 1 provides an overview of Jewish history for the Second Temple period (though some periods are treated more fully in later chapters) and then discusses the main sources. It is important that the reader takes note of where we get our knowledge of the Judaism of this time. There is no magical key to understanding Judaism during this era. We are all dependent on a handful of sources from which most of our knowledge comes. After the introductory chapter, the next four chapters look at various 'currents' or streams within Judaism. By treating them as moving streams we begin to see the dynamic aspect of Jewish history and realize that much of it is produced by the interaction of various movements. So I discuss textual Judaism (Chapter 2), revolutionary Judaism (Chapter 3), eschatological

Judaism (Chapter 4), and the strange phenomenon known as Gnosticism which seems to have Jewish roots (Chapter 5). Together they encompass most facets of Judaism of the time.

What will soon become clear to the reader is that the idea of 'orthodoxy' or a 'state church' is not a good way of looking at Judaism before 70. British readers need to put the model of the Church of England out of mind. There was a centre to the religion: worship at the Jerusalem temple. Most Jews accepted the sacredness of the temple and the general teachings of the Torah. But there was no official orthodoxy (in the Christian sense), for it is clear that there were many interpretations of the Torah and many different views about how to apply the law outside the temple (within the temple, the priests were in control). Thus, each of the Chapters 2–5 tells us about one aspect of Judaism, but as will soon be apparent the various currents are not isolated entities. On the contrary, a single individual may have been a part of more than one current. A study of one particular current helps us to understand one aspect of Judaism, while the study of all four discussed here provides a quite comprehensive picture of Judaism – albeit, a complex picture, like a mosaic with many different parts.

I quote widely from the original sources at different points, both to illustrate my points and to help the reader to become more aware of the source of our knowledge. I usually use the New Jewish Publication Society translation for quotations from the Hebrew Bible (Old Testament). Quotations from the New Testament and the Apocrypha are taken from the New Revised Standard Version. For Philo, Josephus, and the Greek and Roman writers I generally use the Loeb Classical Library. The Dead Sea Scrolls are usually quoted from the translation of Geza Vermes (see the end of Chapter 1). For the Pseudepigrapha, the translations in the *Old Testament Pseudepigrapha* and the *Apocryphal Old Testament* are usually used (again, see the end of Chapter 1). The Nag Hammadi texts in Chapter 5 are quoted from *The Nag Hammadi Library in English*.

This book originated in the Frankland and West Weekend School Lectures given at Birkbeck College on 25–26 March 1995, and were originally published as *An Introduction to First*

Century Judaism (1996). I thank Mr Michael Combermere and Dr Gwen Griffith Dickson for inviting and hosting me, and Professor Michael Knibb of King's College, London, for suggesting my name and chairing the first two lectures. The present version has had a number of revisions, especially in Chapters 1 and 6, and all the bibliographies have been updated. Mrs Jerilyn Sculley has kindly read Chapter 1 from the point of view of the educated lay person. This book is very much the product of teaching early Judaism for many years, especially at the University of Hull but also in America and in various lectures in the UK. To those many students, who have been my willing (for the most part) guinea pigs, I dedicate this book.

L.L.G.
Kingston upon Hull
6 September 2009

OUTLINE OF MAJOR EVENTS

Nehemiah (445 BCE)

PERSIAN PERIOD
(539–331 BCE)

Alexander defeats Darius III (331 BCE)
Death of Alexander (323 BCE)
Period of the Diadochi (323–281 BCE)

EARLY GREEK PERIOD
(331–301 BCE)

Ptolemy II (282–246 BCE)

PTOLEMAIC RULE OF
PALESTINE
(301–200 BCE)

Zenon's tour of Palestine (259 BCE)

Activities of Joseph and Hyrcanus
  Tobiad (late 3rd century BCE)

Antiochus III (223–187 BCE)

SELEUCID RULE OF
PALESTINE
(200–140 BCE)

Antiochus IV (175–164 BCE)

Maccabaean Revolt (168–165 BCE)
Death of Judas (161 BCE)
Jonathan Maccabee (161–143 BCE)
Simon Maccabee (143–135 BCE)
John Hyrcanus I (135–104 BCE)
Aristobulus I (104–103 BCE)
Alexander Jannaeus (103–76 BCE)
Alexandra Salome (76–67 BCE)
Aristobulus II/Hyrcanus II (67–63 BCE)

HASMONAEAN RULE
(140–63 BCE)

Pompey takes Jerusalem (63 BCE)

ROMAN RULE
(63 BCE–)

Herod the Great (40–4 BCE)
Archelaus (4 BCE–6 CE)
Roman province of Judaea (6–41 CE)
Agrippa I (41–44 CE)
Roman province of Judaea (44– CE)

Fall of Jerusalem (70 CE)
Fall of Masada (73 CE)

Jewish revolts in Egypt and Mesopotamia
    (115–117 CE)
Bar Kokhba revolt (132–135 CE)

CHAPTER 1

⟳⟶⟶

INTRODUCTION: HISTORICAL OVERVIEW AND SOURCES

The purpose of this chapter is to orient the reader to the history of the people of Judah and the Jewish Diaspora, for the seven hundred years from the mid-6th century BCE to the end of the Bar Kokhba revolt about 135 of the Common Era, what is often referred to in Jewish history as the Second Temple period. It will give you a broad overview of this period of history and provide a chronological framework of events, since the other chapters are more topical and will deal only with some aspects of the history of Judaism.

1.1 Historical and Religious Background

In this section, you will be given a quick survey of Judahite history from the time of the Israelite monarchy to the period after the fall of the temple and Jerusalem to the Romans. Although the detail of this history may be quite new to many readers, enough information is given to provide a context for Chapters 2–5 which describe 'currents' within Judaism. When you read Chapters 2–5, you should refer to 'Chronological Chart' and then back to this chapter to see how the specific events resonate with events of Jewish history.

1.1.1 The Period of the Israelite and Judahite Monarchies

The origins and early history of Israel are very much debated at the moment (see Grabbe 2007 for a thorough account of this debate and its consequences). Some of this history comes from biblical books that scholarship has not regarded as historical for the past two centuries. For example, the story of the Israelite conquest of Canaan. The story found in the books of Samuel and Kings has often been taken as substantially historical by many scholars until recently. Now, however, there is a good deal of debate about even such major figures as David and Solomon. There is general agreement that we know a fair amount about the history of the kingdoms of Israel and Judah during certain periods, though that information often comes from outside the biblical text. The history of ancient Israel raises some of the same questions about historical knowledge as we shall encounter with the history of the Second Temple, but the subject is too large to debate here and is, in any case, outside the concerns of the present book.

The period of the 'First Temple' (the Israelite and Judahite monarchies) came to an end in 587/586 BCE when the Babylonians conquered Jerusalem, executed some of the royal family and took others captive, and destroyed the temple. Some of the people were also deported, though the actual figures preserved in the biblical literature (e.g. Jeremiah 52) suggest only a minority of the population. Those deported may have been some of the ablest and leading members of the society, but the bulk of the population apparently remained in the land, though many people died in the war and from disease or related causes in the wake of the Babylonian conquest. Judeans had already been deported to Babylonia in the captivity of 597 BCE, and the new deportations added to them. Indications are that this community in Babylonia grew and expanded over time to become a significant Jewish population outside Palestine. Some of those returned in the early Persian period, but evidently the bulk of the deportees and their descendants remained in Babylonia. For the next half century, the Jews in Palestine were evidently in a low state, with Jerusalem desolate and the region administered from Mizpah. This is often referred to as the 'exilic period'. During this time Judah was under the rule of the Neo-Babylonian kings, primarily Nebuchadnezzar, Amel-Marduk, and Nabonidus.

1.1.2 *Persian Rule*

Cyrus the Great conquered Babylon in October 539 BCE. This was the official founding date of the Persian empire which continued for more than two centuries. Some scholars have argued that the Persian period was one of the most productive for Hebrew literature. During these two centuries, earlier Israelite literature and traditions were edited and others were written, or so many scholars think; if they are right, this was one of the most prolific times of Jewish literary activity. The difficulty is that this is a very obscure period in the history of the Jews.

Two biblical books claim to describe the Jews of Palestine in the Persian period; these are Ezra and Nehemiah. We also have the prophetic books of Zechariah (especially chs 1–8) and Haggai. As well be discussed under 'Sources', not everything in these books is credible, but even if we could accept every word of these two books, we would have enough information to write only a fraction of Jewish history during this time. Much of the Persian period is blank for Jewish history, however you look at it. If a good deal of the work of writing and editing the Hebrew Bible went on during this time, it is hardly surprising that we know nothing about it. Yet we are not completely ignorant: for some parts of this 200-year period we have a fair amount of information, and for other parts we have some outline information provided by archaeology and other sources.

As noted in the previous section, many Jews were left in the land by the Babylonians. The population was not large, however, because many had died as a result of the Babylonian conquest and the hardships caused by it. When the Persians defeated the Babylonians and took over their territories, Judah came under Persian rule, but there was no fighting in Palestine, and the Jews were not particularly affected. Over the next decades some Jews returned from Babylonia, though the numbers were probably small, and the temple was rebuilt, probably by about 500 BCE. We then hear little until the middle of the fifth century BCE when Nehemiah was allowed to return to Jerusalem and rebuild the walls of the city. Why it was necessary to rebuild the walls at this time is not clear, though there is no evidence that they were needed for defence. (If they had been needed for defence, they would not have been left in disrepair for so long.) The existence of walls would, however, make it easier for the leaders to have oversight of and control the population, as when Nehemiah shut up the gates of the city on the Sabbath (Nehemiah 13.15–22). It looks as if this was Nehemiah's goal: to make the people conform to a religious ideology of his own. It is clear from the book of Nehemiah that many resisted this aim, though as the duly appointed governor he could enforce conformity. As soon as he left, however, many ceased to follow his dictates (Nehemiah 6.17–19; 13).

The persona of Ezra is a puzzle. He is presented in Ezra 7 as not only as a scribe and bringer of the law but also as a powerful governor, even satrap, who had great authority over the whole region of the Persian empire west of the Euphrates. Yet his actions in Ezra 8–10 do not always show him as a powerful figure but almost as a weak one who needs others to suggest what to do. Furthermore, he brings enormous wealth with him to Jerusalem which is far in excess of anything that the Persians might have bestowed upon an important temple in Babylonia, much less the temple of a small people on the edge of the empire. There is also the problem that Ezra is not the primary lawgiver in other traditions. For example, Ben Sira 49.11–13 ascribes the main activities in Persian Judah to Joshua, Zerubbabel, and Nehemiah, while 2 Maccabees 2.13 makes Nehemiah the main collector of scriptural writings; in neither case is Ezra mentioned at all. It seems likely that the Torah (the Pentateuch or the first Five Books of Moses) was composed late in the Persian period, but by whom and how it was promulgated is not presently known. We know that a high priest named Jehohanan was in office not long after this, from a letter preserved among the Elephantine papyri (see below). Nehemiah had died or returned to Susa, and the high priest was once again in charge.

We also have documents from a Jewish military colony living on the island of Elephantine in Aswan area of the Nile in the late fifth century BCE. They had their own temple, in spite of the fact that this is forbidden in the Pentateuch, but there is no evidence that they had the Pentateuch, even though they evidently observed certain tradition of Jewish laws and customs. About 410 BCE their temple was destroyed by a mob of local Egyptians, instituted by the priest of the god Chnum. Since Chnum was a ram-headed god, it may be that they were offended by the Passover celebrations. The Elephantine Jewish community appealed to the high priest and the Jerusalem community for support (the letter in the Aramaic *lingua franca* of the Persian empire) is preserved, but we have no indication that the high priest replied to the letter. Unfortunately, the Aramaic documents relating to the Jewish colony come to an end in Elephantine about that time, and we do not know the fate of the community (documents continued into the Greek period but do not relate clearly to the Jewish military colony).

As for the Jews in Palestine, our sources also come to an end by 400 BCE, and we have no further information except for archaeology, though we do know something of the history of events in the general region. The Egyptians rebelled against Persian rule during the fourth century, and we read in Greek histories of clashes between the Persian army and the Egyptians. Phoenicia on the coast was a staging area for ships transporting troops to fight and for naval bases supporting the military ships. Since Judah was isolated up in the hill country, however, we do not have any evidence that they were affected in a significant way by these events. From all we can tell they continued to live much as they had before and began to recover their economy and prosperity.

1.1.3 *The Greek Conquest and Ptolemaic Rule*

The next major events affecting the Jews around Jerusalem occurred with the coming of the Greeks. In 334 BCE Alexander led a Greek army against the Persian empire. Darius III failed to stop him at Issus in Asia Minor the next year. Most of Syria submitted to the Greeks at this point, except for two cities: Tyre and Gaza. Alexander besieged Tyre and took it after seven months. He then moved down the coast to Gaza and took it, before marching into Egypt. There is a legend that he also came to

Jerusalem to destroy it but instead prostrated himself before the high priest. This deserves little credence – the historians of Alexander were very interested in such things and would have reported it – but it was probably during Alexander's progress south along the coast that a representative of the Jewish people came to him and made the necessary submission to this new conqueror. In doing so, the Jews would have been just another small country or ethnic group of the many within the Persian empire. The final defeat of Darius III came in 331 BCE. Alexander himself died in 323, and for the next 40 years his generals (the *Diadochi* or 'Successors') fought over his empire. In 301 BCE an agreement gave Syro-Palestine to Seleucus I, but Ptolemy I made a quick excursion from Egypt and seized the region. This began a century of Ptolemaic rule of the Jews.

The early part of the Greek period is not much better known than the Persian period. We know little during the 40-year period of the Diadochi or the first couple of decades of Ptolemaic rule. A few pieces of miscellaneous information may be fitted in somewhere, but their dating and even their authenticity is very much up in the air. Ptolemy (I?) took Jerusalem on the Sabbath day (when? why? what were the consequences?), and the high priest (and governor?) Ezechias (Hezekiah) came to Ptolemy, bringing a large group of settlers with him (according to Josephus, *Against Apion* 1.22 §§ 185, 187):

> Among these (he says) was Ezechias, a chief priest of the Jews, a man of about sixty-six years of age, highly esteemed by his country-men, intellectual, and moreover an able speaker and unsurpassed as a man of business. Yet (he adds) the total number of Jewish priests who receive a tithe of the revenue and administer public affairs is about fifteen hundred.

It is in the early part of the Hellenistic period that new sources of information start to become available to supplement and form a corrective to the literary sources. Some are in the form of inscriptions and economic documents. Not too many of these are preserved, though the few we have are valuable. The most important source revealed by archaeology is the *Zenon papyri*. This is the archive belonging to Zenon who was the agent

of Apollonius, Ptolemy II's minister of finance. In 259 BCE
Zenon went on a year-long tour of Palestine and southern Syria
on his master's business. During the course of that tour he met
and dealt with a variety of officials in Palestine, and he continued to correspond with some of them for a number of years
afterward. Thus, his personal archive constitutes an important
collection of letters and documents which give us a window into
the society of Judah and the surrounding region at that time.

One of the figures we meet in the pages of Zenon's corre-
spondence is Tobias who was head of a military colony (called
a 'cleruchy') just over the Jordan river. He was a local leader or
sheik of considerable power and influence whom the Ptolemaic
government made use of in its financial and political administration. Although Tobias' cleruchy was made up of soldiers from
a variety of ethnic groups, he himself was Jewish and apparently
from a family which had constituted a local power for perhaps
several centuries. Some of Tobias' descendents evidently went
on to make their mark in Jewish history in the next century
or so.

Josephus (*Antiquities* 12.4.1–11 §§157–236) reports a semi-
legendary story of Joseph who was Tobias' son or grandson.
Joseph was the nephew of the high priest Onias II. For some
reason, Onias was refusing to pay a particular sum of tribute to
his Ptolemaic overlords. We are not told why, but scholars have
inferred that Onias was pro-Seleucid. As noted above, Palestine
and Syria had been assigned to the Seleucid empire in 301 BCE,
but the Ptolemies took it over and would not yield it. Thus,
throughout the entire third century the Seleucids fought a
series of 'Syrian Wars' against the Ptolemies to take southern
Syria and Palestine under their rule. They did so with a certain
legal claim though, as so often in international politics, might
makes right and possession is nine-tenths of the law. The Ptolemies had control of Syro-Palestine and aimed to keep it, but
they had to defend it periodically with military force. Onias II
may have thought that the Seleucids were about to succeed and
took the opportunity to withhold the expected tribute.

Whatever Onias' motives, Joseph Tobiad used his actions as
an occasion to advance himself in the eyes of both the Jewish

community and the Ptolemaic government: he went to the Ptolemaic ruler, apologized for the actions of the high priest, and paid the tribute. Joseph then bid for and obtained the tax farming rights to the whole region. The Greeks and later the Romans found that the most effective way to collect taxes on goods and sales was by selling the rights to private individuals ('tax farmers') for a specified sum. The would-be tax farmers had to bid against one another, and the right to collect the tax went to the highest bidder. By shrewd bidding and ruthless collection Joseph made himself rich and, at the same time, a powerful figure who was close to the Ptolemaic rulers. It is doubtful that he was tax farmer over the whole region, as the semi-legendary account claims, because we would probably have heard of him in other sources, but he was probably a powerful figure locally, perhaps over Judah or perhaps even a larger region in Palestine.

After some two decades of success, his youngest son Hyrcanus outmanoeuvred his father and took away the tax farming rights from him. We know of this Hyrcanus Tobiad because he had a large sum of money on deposit at the Jerusalem temple (2 Maccabees 3.11). Joseph and Hyrcanus' other brothers were incensed at this but could do little about it. However, things turned their way after not too long a time had passed because the Seleucids finally took Palestine away from the Ptolemies in 200 BCE. It looks as if the Tobiad family became split along political lines, with Joseph and the majority of his sons deciding that the future lay with the Seleucids, whereas Hyrcanus remained loyal to the Ptolemies. When Antiochus III defeated Ptolemy V in 200 BCE and finally obtained Syro-Palestine, Hyrcanus was left high and dry. He retired to the ancestral home in the Transjordanian region and lived there by plundering the local Arab tribes for the next quarter of a century until his death when Antiochus IV came to the throne.

1.1.4 *The Seleucids and the 'Hellenistic Reform'*

This section and the next one will relate the 'Hellenistic reform' and the events preceding the Maccabean revolt in a good deal of detail. The reason is the importance of these events for subsequent Jewish history and for scholarly debate. The Seleucid ruler Antiochus III is known in history as Antiochus the Great. He suffered a major defeat at Raphia in 217 BCE fighting against the Ptolemies but came back in less than 20 years to gain the goal his ancestors had claimed for a century: in 200 BCE he took Syro-Palestine. The Seleucid empire now stretched to the borders of Egypt. The Jews themselves seem to have been by and large pro-Seleucid and had opened the gates of Jerusalem to Antiochus. There must have been some fighting in the city because damage was done, as mentioned by Ben Sira (50.1). Antiochus rewarded the Jerusalem establishment by granting the traditional right to practise their religion and by remitting taxes for a short period of time to enable them to repair the damage to their city (*Antiquities* 12.3.3–4 §§ 138–46; quoted at 2.5). The change to Seleucid rule looked as if it would be good for the Jews.

Encouraged by his success against Egypt Antiochus III went on to spread his empire to the north. Alas, at this very same time the Romans were extending their influence into the East. Antiochus was defeated at Magnesia in 190 BCE and required to pay heavy war indemnities, to send one of his sons to Rome as a hostage, and also to hamstring his war elephants. He lived only a few more years and was succeeded by his son Seleucus IV in 187 BCE.

A strange episode took place under Seleucus, if there is any truth in 2 Maccabees 3. Seleucus was informed that a good deal of money was kept in the Jerusalem temple treasury, so he sent one of his officers to confiscate it for the royal coffers. This seems not to have happened, though. According to 2 Maccabees, this was because of a miracle in which an angel of God suddenly intervened. Exactly what happened is unclear, since few of us are willing to take the account of 2 Maccabees at face value. Why would Seleucus attempt to seize the temple money? One of the reasons seems to be that a large deposit of Hyrcanus Tobiad's was being kept there (2 Maccabees 3:11) and, as noted above, Hyrcanus was probably pro-Ptolemy and thus regarded as an enemy of the state by Seleucus. Why Seleucus' minister failed to take the money remains a matter of speculation, assuming that the story is not sheer legend.

When Seleucus IV died in 175 BCE, his brother Antiochus was just returning from Rome where he had been a hostage. Seleucus' own son (also called Antiochus) was still a minor, and the older Antiochus took the throne as Antiochus IV. Contrary to the impression given by many surveys and introductions to this period of Jewish history, Antiochus did not immediately begin to 'Hellenize' all the peoples under his rule nor to force the Jewish people to conform to some sort of mad scheme he had cooked up. He was not a cultural zealot who wanted to impose Greek forms on the Near Eastern peoples, nor was he demented or deluded. On the contrary, Antiochus was like most rulers in being interested in two things: money and power. He was also evidently a very able ruler, though history was against him. He hoped to expand his territory and influence like his father had done but – also like his father – he had to reckon with the power of Rome.

The question of Hellenization is a complicated one, and it is too often reduced to a caricature. Hellenization was a centuries-long process of synthesis and diversification. It was not the simple imposition of Greek culture on the natives; indeed, the Greeks on the whole did not impose their culture but rather jealously preserved their 'superior' political and cultural position in Near Eastern society. It was mainly the natives who sought to gain status and advantage by learning Greek and adopting Greek customs. The Near Eastern peoples adopted Greek elements that were useful to them, and sometimes adapted them to their own needs as well. Also, a lot of Greek influence spread by osmosis rather than by deliberate acts of 'cultural imperialism'. The lower section of the administration was mainly composed of native peoples, and much of the work of the bureaucracy was carried on in bilingual mode – Greek by no means ousted cuneiform in Babylonia or Demotic in Egypt or Aramaic in Syro-Palestine; however, those who could gain a Greek education – and this was mainly the upper-class of the indigenous peoples – usually found that it conferred benefits. In time Greek identity became more a matter of language and education than of ethnic origin, but this took many decades.

Hellenistic culture was a synthesis of Greek and Near Eastern. Greek forms did not replace native culture; they rather supplemented it. That is, Greek forms and Near Eastern forms flourished side by side, and only gradually did they begin to intermix in a syncretistic sort of way. To be Hellenistic was not to be Greek; Hellenization was *sui generis* – it was a true synthesis of Greek and Near Eastern into something new. Indeed, much that was characteristic of the Hellenistic empires had more in common with the old Near Eastern empires than with classical Greece. The adoption of Greek elements varied greatly, with the upper-class taking on more of the Greek and the masses of the people borrowing less. Nevertheless, Greek influence percolated through the entire culture as time progressed so that much which came from the Greeks was no longer recognized as being borrowed but was thoroughly assimilated. The Jews were no exception to this process but a full part of it.

So Antiochus did not set out to be an apostle of Greek culture. Rather he spent the first five years of his reign consolidating his power and resources, then he launched the first of his campaigns to extend his empire. This was where his mind was focused, and none of his actions suggest differently. During this time, however, the Jewish high priestly family developed an internal rivalry. The high priest Onias III, the son of Simon II, had a brother named Jason (his Greek, with Joshua his Hebrew name). Jason went to Antiochus and offered him money to be given the high priesthood. The amount offered was 440 talents of silver. The wording of 2 Maccabees 4.8, which gives us this information, suggests that it represented an increase in the annual tribute. Antichus readily agreed, and why not? Jason was evidently acceptable to him, it was no skin off his nose as to who was Jewish high priest, and he got much-needed cash for his coffers.

Jason also asked for something else, for which he paid an additional 150 talents (apparently per annum). This was the opportunity to build a gymnasium, enrol the inhabitants of Jerusalem as citizens, and draw up an ephebate list. 2 Maccabees 4 which describes this is not explicit, but it would have been obvious to readers of the time: Jason he had obtained permission to make Jerusalem into a *polis* or Greek city. The government of such a city was considered to be in the hands of the citizens, so citizenship was very important and a considerable privilege. Not everyone who lived in the city was a citizen. Jason was given the right to draw up the citizenship lists, and one suspects that those enrolled paid for the prerogative. The youth of the city were also added to lists of potential citizens called the 'ephebate' and went through a process of formal initiation. The gymnasium was not just a place of physical exercise. It was the educational and cultural centre of the city. The young men of the city would be educated here in language and literature, as well as physical sports and military skills, preparing them for citizenship. It also served as a social centre where people would gather to talk and watch the athletic contests. Building a gymnasium was essential to establish Jerusalem as a Greek foundation.

Yet this did not mean an essential change to the Jewish religion. According to 2 Maccabees 4, Jason was an exceedingly wicked man. We can agree that he usurped the priesthood from his brother, but beyond that we have no evidence of any breach of Jewish religious law. This is quite evident when we read 2 Maccabees 4 carefully: the narrator uses much emotive language, but he cannot point to any specific transgression of law. On the contrary, the temple continued to function, the required daily offering was offered up as usual, people brought their sin-, free-will, and well-being offerings as they had always done. Indeed, it was not in Jason's interest to make substantial changes to the cult because this was his financial and power base. He had to take the people with him, and it seems clear that he did. All indications are that the people of Jerusalem as a whole supported his 'Hellenistic reform'.

One often reads that 'the pious were outraged' by what Jason did. Unfortunately, such statements are sheer fantasy. We have no indication of any active opposition whatsoever to the Hellenistic reform. It *might* have been that some people did not like it; it would be surprising if everyone approved. Nevertheless, we have no evidence of any opposition – the sources are silent on the subject. This is not accidental, because at a later stage there was opposition to certain actions. This shows that the people were not indifferent to anything which threatened their religion. The silence with regard to Jason is eloquent testimony to his remaining true to the existing religious cult. His changes were political, not religious.

There were some changes that affected the Jews, inevitably, because this brought Jerusalem and its people into the wider Hellenistic world. For example, when some games were held in Tyre and attended by many foreign representatives, Jason sent a sum of money in honour of the celebrations. According to 2 Maccabees 4.18–20 Jason sent the money for pagan sacrifices. The money was not used for such sacrifices, however, but was instead spent on warships. The text claims that this was the decision of the messengers carrying the money to Tyre, but this is incredible. Jason would have chosen his messengers carefully, knowing that they carried a considerable sum. It is most likely that the money was not meant for sacrifices in the first place but to be spent on triremes – and this was simply an anti-Jason calumny.

Yet 1 Maccabees 1.15 claims that some Jews attempted to remove the marks of circumcision. The reason for this would have been that athletes competed in the nude, and some Jewish athletes were embarrassed by their circumcision. No doubt there were a few examples of this happening, but it is unlikely to have affected many. There were not many Jewish international athletes, and any such operation to become 'uncircumcised' would have been quite painful (see the description in the medical writer Celsus 7.25.1). It would have taken considerable motivation to undergo such as process. The number of those disguising circumcision was likely to have been very small.

Jason's new reforms did not last long. After about three years, a man from another priestly family did the same trick as Jason; Menelaus (whose brother Simon was 'captain [*prostatēs*] of the temple') was sent as a messenger to Antiochus IV. He took the opportunity to proffer Antiochus an even larger bribe than Jason had done. Once again Antiochus saw no reason to refuse such a generous offer, and Jason was deposed in favour

of Menelaus. Menelaus' reach was greater than his grasp, however, and he failed to pay the amount he promised. Considering
that he offered an addition 300 talents on top of what Jason was
paying, it is unlikely that Judah could produce so much surplus
wealth, especially if it was meant to be an annual payment.

Menelaus tried to solve his problem by bribing some of
Antiochus' ministers, allegedly by selling some of the golden
temple vessels. The truth of this allegation is difficult to judge
now, though it is possible this was only a rumour. What is important is that the people believed it, and they reacted strongly to
what they regarded as a breach of religious law. They collected
in the streets in protest. Menelaus had gone to Antioch, leaving
his brother Lysimachus in charge. Lysimachus brought out a
large number of his own men to break up the riot; instead he
was killed and his followers routed. Then the Council sent a
delegation to protest to Antiochus. Remember that this was
the Council (*gerousia*) who governed the 'Hellenistic' city of
Jerusalem founded by Jason. In other words, it was evidently
some of the so-called 'Hellenizers' who dispatched this mission
to Antiochus to protest a violation of religious law. As said
before, the people were very concerned about the temple and
the proper conduct of the cult. The fact that they supported
the initial Hellenistic reform of Jason did not affect their view
of the Jewish religion which they still strongly supported. The
'Hellenistic reform' was not a matter of religion but of culture.
By means of further bribes, however, Menelaus escaped any
punishment and retained his office.

1.1.5 The Maccabaean Revolt

It was a couple of years after Menelaus took over the high priesthood, in late 170 or early 169 BCE, that Antiochus proceeded
with the plan for which he had spent five years preparing. He
invaded Egypt (though in response to an Egyptian attack). It
may be that he was not trying for direct conquest but a dynastic
change favourable to himself. If so, he succeeded. Ptolemy VI
was defeated and then agreed to marry Antiochus' daughter.

Antiochus accomplished all his goals and returned in triumph with a great many spoils. Although the accounts in both 1 and 2 Maccabees are plainly confused, it seems that it was while on his way back from Egypt that he visited Jerusalem, was taken into the temple itself by Menelaus (in violation of the law), and raided the temple treasury to the tune of 1800 talents.

In a short period of time, the rival figures of the Ptolemaic royal family undid Antiochus' grand vision. Therefore, only about a year later Antiochus felt the need to advance against Egypt once again in the spring of 168. This time things did not go so well as before. The Romans had been watching Antiochus and were concerned that he not extend his influence further. A Roman delegation was in the region. Waiting until they had received the news of the battle of Pydna, which the Romans won, the delegation met Antiochus and demanded that he withdraw. He had no choice, for he was not prepared to confront Rome. In July 168 he started back to Syria. In the meantime, events in Judah had come to a head. Jason had heard a rumour that Antiochus was dead and seized the apparent opportunity to attack Menelaus and take back the office which he had stolen fair and square. He entered Jerusalem with his followers, and Menelaus was forced to take refuge in the akra (the citadel).

When Antiochus heard this, he interpreted it as a revolt and sent an army to Jerusalem to sort things out (he apparently did not come there himself). Events from then on become somewhat uncertain because the data given in 1 and 2 Maccabees do not always make sense. It is clear that Jerusalem was taken and the followers of Jason driven away. Allegedly 40,000 inhabitants of Jerusalem were killed and another 40,000 enslaved – though there were hardly so many Jerusalemites at that time! A series of measures followed, some of them inexplicable: governors were put in charge of Judah, a logical enactment for a rebellious province. But then Apollonius the captain of Mysian soldiers was sent to take the city (why?), which he did even though the city was itself peaceful (so why take it by force?), and killed many Jews (how, when they had all been killed or enslaved months earlier?). Finally, an Athenian was sent to suppress Jewish worship. The daily sacrifice was stopped, and the temple was polluted with an alien cult, apparently in December 168 BCE (so I have argued, though many standard works make it a year later).

The whole incident is very puzzling. Antiochus had interpreted Jason's attack as a revolt, but he had put it down and had put governors in charge of the province. So why send Apollonius to attack Jerusalem *again*? And, especially, why suppress the religion – an unheard-of way of dealing with a revolt in any case, and doubly peculiar here since the revolt had been put down months before? The cause or causes of the Maccabaean revolt have been one of the most perplexing in Jewish history. Although one often reads facile statements about Hellenization or religious syncretism or other simplistic solutions, there is no clearly defined reason for what happened. A variety of serious and sober suggestions have been made, and some of these may be on the right track. Nevertheless, a solution which would command a consensus of specialists has not yet been proposed.

It is hardly surprising that this attempt to blot out traditional Jewish worship evoked a reaction. Exactly how the resistance began is still a matter of speculation. It would be reasonable to assume that it was initiated independently in several different quarters. Our sources emphasize the place of the Maccabean family, but that is probably not the full story. What we do know is that Judas Maccabee and his brothers eventually secured leadership of the resistance. The books of 1 and 2 Maccabees recount a series of military encounters. We shall not look at those in detail, though in several cases important victories were won. We can sum up by saying that over a period of three years, the Maccabee brothers and their followers won sufficient victories against the Seleucids to take back the temple and purify it.

This success was not miraculous, because it can be explained by normal military measures, but it was unusual. The result was that Antiochus rescinded his decree of religious suppression. The Jews once again had their temple and the right to worship as they chose. For many Jews this was sufficient; their religion

was safe, and they ceased fighting. Not so the Maccabees. Whatever their initial reasons for fighting, they had now developed a
desire to secure independence for Judah as a nation once more.
This was a bold dream, for Judah had not been independent for
many centuries. For many Jews this must have been an absurd
notion, since support for the Maccabees dropped drastically.

Judah himself was killed about 161, and the Maccabaean
resistance went into a decade of eclipse. Jonathan succeeded
his brother, but he and his followers were on the run from
the Seleucid army much of the time. The breakthrough came
when rivalry developed for the Seleucid throne: two separate
dynasties claimed the throne and put up pretenders who fought
against each other for another half century and more. This
allowed Jonathan to be courted by both claimants to the throne
and to support the one from whom he felt he could gain
the most. He was thus declared high priest and a friend of the
Seleucid king. This was important, because now the high priest
was in a different family from the traditional one (the Oniads).
Some Jews would never accept the Hasmonaean high priesthood. Jonathan met his death at the hand of one of the rivals
when he made a political miscalculation, and his brother Simon
became leader in 143 BCE.

1.1.6 *The Hasmonaean Dynasty*

The Maccabean dynasty is traditionally referred to as the
'Hasmonaeans', after an ancestor. Hasmonaean rule can perhaps
be formally dated from Simon's rule (143–135 BCE). He negoti-
ated with the Seleucid ruler Demetrius II who made some fairly
extensive promises to him. Thus, 1 Maccabees can state that in
the first year of his reign, 'the yoke of the Gentiles was removed
from Israel' (13:41–42). In the third year of his reign, an assembly of the Jews made a declaration of freedom which reflected
the aspirations of the Jews, if not quite the reality (1 Maccabees
14:27–45, NRSV):

> On the eighteenth day of Elul [August-September], in the one
> hundred seventy-second year [of the Seleucid era], which is the

third year of the great high priest Simon, in Asaramel . . . . The Jews and their priests have resolved that Simon should be their leader and high priest forever, until a trustworthy prophet should arise, and that he should be governor over them and that he should take charge of the sanctuary and appoint officials over its tasks and over the country and the weapons and the strongholds, and that he should take charge of the sanctuary, and that he should be obeyed by all, and that all contracts in the country should be written in his name, and that he should be clothed in purple and wear gold.

In some ways, Jonathan had already become the de facto Jewish ruler, with the office of high priest, while the title of king was not to be taken for another 40 years. Yet it is this declaration about 140 BCE more than any other which allows one to speak formally of the Hasmonaean dynasty and Judah as an independent nation.

Simon is said to have finally expelled the Seleucid troops from the Akra, the central citadel of Jerusalem. This removed the last symbol of Seleucid rule from the country. Nevertheless, the Seleucids had not given up their claims. Antiochus VII made demands on Simon and then attacked him when he refused to comply. Since Simon was too aged to lead in battle, his sons led the army and defeated Antiochus; however, Simon was treacherously slain by his son-in-law.

Simon's son John Hyrcanus (I) was a long-lived ruler (135–104 BCE) who began the expansion of Judaean territory. Even in the early part of his reign, he was not free from Seleucid interference, but the continued rivalry for the Seleucid throne freed John to do much as he wanted through most of his reign. He ceased to pay tribute to the Seleucids and took the important Samaritan cities of Shechem and Samaria. He also conquered Idumaea and forced the inhabitants to convert to Judaism. Surprisingly, they seem to have remained loyal to this new religion for the most part, as indicated by later references.

Aristobulus I (104–103 BCE) was Hyrcanus' eldest son. He lived only a year but is credited with being the first to assume the title 'king'. He also conquered the territory of Ituraea in southern Lebanon and forcibly converted it to Judaism.

Alexander Jannaeus (103–76 BCE) was the brother of Aristobulus and had been imprisoned by him when he died. Aristobulus' widow released Jannaeus, offered him the throne, and married him. Jannaeus turned out to be another long-lived and dynamic ruler like John Hyrcanus. Despite hard work and many successes, however, his reign was a troubled one. He further expanded the territory left to him by Hyrcanus, but a considerable opposition developed among the Jews themselves. This led to the incident about 88 BCE when his opponents invited Demetrius III, one of a number of claimants to the Seleucid throne at this time, to attack him. Demetrius invaded with many Jews in his army; he and Jannaeus fought to a standstill, and it looked as if Jannaeus might be defeated if the war continued. However, in the night after the main battle many of the Jews switched sides (probably because of concern that if Jannaeus was routed, Demetrius might take over control of Judah). Demetrius realized he had lost his advantage and retired, leaving Jannaeus firmly on the throne. Jannaeus now turned his attention to his enemies, crucifying 800 of them in the arena while he and his concubines feasted and watched their death agonies. A large number of those opposed to him fled the country.

Among Jannaeus' opponents were the Pharisees, at least according to one account given by Josephus. Allegedly on his deathbed, Jannaeus told his wife Alexandra Salome to make peace with them. This story sounds apocryphal, and there is a certain air of contrivance in the whole account of the death of Jannaeus and the succession of Alexandra. Yet there still may be a central truth to the story. What is clear is that Alexandra took the throne (76–67 BCE), one of the few female rulers in Israel's history, and the Pharisees dominated her rule. It is one of the few times in which the Pharisees were able to influence the ruler and have their religious laws enforced on the people (see further at 2.6.3).

Alexandra appointed her elder son Hyrcanus II to the office of high priest. His younger brother Aristobulus II was determined to have the rule and rebelled even while Alexandra was still ruler. As soon as she died, he seized the throne, and

Hyrcanus agreed to be contented with only being high priest. Hyrcanus had an advisor named Antipater who had been the governor of Idumaea. Whether he was himself Idumaean is a matter of debate, but the Idumaeans in any case had been converted to Judaism by John Hyrcanus. Antipater encouraged Hyrcanus not to give up his claims to the throne; eventually Hyrcanus fled to Aretas III, king of the Nabataeans, and returned with an army. He defeated Aristobulus and besieged him in Jerusalem. The Roman general Pompey was in the region of Syria fighting the Armenians and sent his lieutenant to investigate what was happening in Judaea. Both Hyrcanus and Aristobulus appealed to him for support.

Pompey prevaricated about making a decision (allegedly hoping for each side to pay higher bribes), and Aristobulus finally marched off. Pompey pursued him, and he surrendered. However, his followers closed the city of Jerusalem to Pompey's forces. The Romans besieged the city and finally took it in 63 BCE. The priests continued with the temple cult even while fighting took place around them, and many were killed. Pompey himself went into the Holy of Holies, but the next day he ordered the priests to repurify the temple and resume the cult. He did not loot or harm the temple itself. But the Hasmonaean kingdom had come to an end – almost exactly a century after the temple was restored under Judas Maccabaeus.

1.1.7 The Roman Yoke

Pompey's conquest of Jerusalem must have been a terrible blow to many Jews. Judah had been an independent nation for long enough that its position as a small subordinate province had been lost from living memory. To come once again under foreign domination went against the theological views of many: they were God's chosen people – they were not destined to have Gentiles rule over them. Much of the land gained by conquest under Hasmonaean rule was taken away, creating hardship for the Jewish settlers who were now forced out, and Judah returned to being a small territory under foreign rule, this time under a Roman governor. The one consolation (if it was a consolation) is that the high priest and former king Hyrcanus and his advisor Antipater had important places in the new government structure. Antipater was a formidable leader and an astute politician. Hyrcanus is usually presented as being completely in his shadow, which may be a correct analysis but the biased nature of the sources must not be forgotten.

The new province of Judaea and its leaders became caught up in the internecine warfare of the Late Roman Republic. Pompey himself died at the hands of Antony and Julius Caesar in 48 BCE. The author of the *Psalms of Solomon* (2:29–33) took grim satisfaction in this humiliation and death of the conqueror of Jerusalem:

> Delay not, O God, to bring recompense upon their heads,
> To change the pride of the dragon into dishonour.
> And I did not wait long before God showed me his body,
> Stabbed, on the mountains of Egypt,
> Esteemed of less account than the least on land and sea –
> His body, carried about on the waves in great ignominy,
> With none to bury him, because he had rejected him in dishonour.
> He did not consider that he was man,
> Nor did he consider the end.
> He said, I will be lord of land and sea;
> And he did not recognise that God is great,
> Mighty in his great strength.
>   [Translation from Sparks (ed.) 1984]

Antipater and Hyrcanus came out of the event well. They provided much needed aid to Caesar in his invasion of Egypt and were duly rewarded with Roman citizenship. Hyrcanus was declared *ethnarch* of the Jews. (It is probably from this period that anti-Semitism began to develop in Egypt, because the Jews were seen as having assisted the Romans in defeating Egypt.)

Antipater took the opportunity to introduce his two sons to positions of authority in the governmental structure, making the elder Phasael governor of Judaea and Herod governor of Galilee. Both proved to be capable, energetic, and zealous administrators, but it seems that the younger Herod was the more impressive. Among their duties was to raise a war chest for the Romans to pay for an earlier unsuccessful expedition against Parthia. Antipater was poisoned by rivals in the mid-40s, leaving Phasael and Herod to avenge his death (which they did).

Phasael and Herod were worthy successors of their father. In the next phase of the Roman civil war, they actually supported Cassius against Antony and Octavian who were on the winning side, but they do not seem to have suffered for it. When Antony came to establish his rule over the Eastern Mediterranean in 42 BCE, he made Herod and Phasael both tetrarchs, despite a delegation of leading Jews who accused the sons of Antipater of governing the country instead of Hyrcanus. Indeed, Hyrcanus backed Herod and Phasael in this episode.

In 40 BCE the Parthians invaded Syria-Palestine. With them was Antigonus the son of Aristobulus II who still had designs on gaining the Hasmonaean throne. Jerusalem was besieged. Phasael was captured through a ruse and committed suicide. Herod realized he was in a desperate situation. He fled secretly at night, left his family protected in the desert fortress of Masada, and made his way to Rome. He met Antony and Octavian who brought him before the Senate. He was declared king of Judaea and promised help in driving out the Parthians and retaking Jerusalem. Herod once more demonstrated what in many ways became the hallmark of his life – he turned disaster into advantage.

1.1.8 The Reign of Herod the Great

The Parthians did not remain long in Palestine; perhaps they always intended their occupation of the Syria-Palestine to be a temporary measure. Antigonus remained stubbornly in Jerusalem and was besieged by Herod. The city fell in 37 BCE, and Antigonus was executed. Herod was now king de facto, not just de jure. He had a thorn in his side, however: Cleopatra queen of Egypt. Although her influence with Antony was not absolute, she often got her way, and she made many demands with regard to Herod and his territory. Antony often granted her wishes, though he seems to have realized how valuable an ally Herod could be; otherwise, Cleopatra might have had him deposed.

Herod's troubles came to an abrupt end in 31 BCE with the battle of Actium in which the forces of Mark Antony and Cleopatra confronted those of Octavian. Antony and Cleopatra lost, and both sailed to Egypt. This only delayed the inevitable for a brief period of time. In one stroke Herod's chief enemy and chief ally were removed. This time he was on the losing side. However, through good fortune or – more likely – astute political manoeuvring, Herod was fighting the Nabataeans at the time and did not participate in Actium. His response to the new order was characteristic of him: he sailed to Rhodes and boldly came before Octavian. He candidly admitted having backed the wrong side in Antony but, laying his crown before Octavian, expressed his willingness to support him and to be a useful ally. Octavian was a shrewd leader and realized the value of retaining Herod on his side. But perhaps he also saw in the chutzpah of the young Jewish king something of himself. He accepted Herod's offer of loyalty.

For the next 20 years Herod's reign was primarily a success. He had the backing of Rome and was on close terms with the family of the Roman emperor. His status as client king or friendly king gave him autonomy in his own territory. (For this reason, it is unlikely that Roman taxes were collected in his kingdom, though he made many generous gifts to Octavian and to various cities and officials in the Roman Empire.) This period saw many large building projects, including the new city of Caesarea on the coast, palaces at Herodium and Cypros on the Jordan, refurbishment of Masada, construction of the old city of Samaria into Sabaste, and many projects in Greece and other areas outside his own territory. The crown of his building projects, however, was `Herod's temple'. The temple destroyed by Nebuchadnezzar had been rebuilt in the early Persian period. There is some evidence from archaeology that further changes were made during the period of Hasmonaean rule. What Herod did was only refurbishment in a strict sense, since the old temple was altered and redone only a piece at a time, and at no time was it closed to worshipers. Yet the end product was for practical purposes a new temple, a magnificent structure which paled by comparison the previous temples.

The last years of Herod were beset by many problems. A breach developed with Augustus over a conflict with the Nabataeans. Herod was blamed (probably wrongly) for attacking the Nabataeans. Rome allowed client kings basic autonomy in their own internal affairs, but they did not tolerate unauthorized conflicts between client nations. The contretemps between Herod and Nabataea was eventually settled and Herod restored to favour with Augustus, but it took several years. A chief source of difficulties was Herod's own family. He executed his first wife Mariamme for adultery sometime around 30 BCE, along with his uncle Joseph. Then toward the end of his reign he had several of his sons executed for alleged conspiracy to kill him and take the throne (probably with good reason in some of the cases). He finally died of an atrocious disease in 4 BCE.

Herod has been infamous in history. Some of this reputation is deserved and some of it is not. He was a determined ruler who held on to power despite some major adversities and setbacks. Several times he came close to deposition and even death, yet he always won through in the end. He could not have done this without being ruthless when necessary, and he clearly tolerated no opposition. But in this he not different from the other rulers of the time, including the Hasmonaean rulers that some of Herod's subjects harkened back to. On the other hand, he did many services for the Jews. His taxes were tolerable and he remitted them during times of famine, his building projects brought prestige and employment, the new temple became a major site of pilgrimage, and he lived as a Jew and defended Jewish worship outside Palestine (e.g. lobbying for Jews in Asia Minor to be allowed to remit the annual religious tax to Jerusalem). The economic situation he created in Judaea during his reign was beneficial to Jews as a whole.

Thus, Herod had his faults, but his reign was also characterized by many good points. Any evaluation must consider both sides of the question. One thing he probably was *not* guilty of was the 'slaughter of the innocents'. This is a legend reported only by the writer of Matthew 2:16–18 and has no basis in anything known from the history of that time. No other source mentions it, not even Josephus (who despised Herod), much less the Gospel of Luke, as they almost certainly would have had it taken place.

1.1.9 A Roman Province Once Again

After Herod's death, several of his sons by various wives rushed to Rome to claim his throne. At the same time, a delegation from the people came before Augustus to plead for direct Roman rule. The delegation did not get their way at the time, for Herod's son Archelaus was allowed to govern Judaea (though without the title of king), while two of his half-brothers were made tetrarchs, Herod Antipas over Galilee and Perea and Philip over territories to the north and east of Galilee. However, in 6 CE Archelaus was banished for misrule and Judaea made into a Roman province once again.

As soon as direct Roman rule was imposed, a census was taken in order to instate Roman taxation. Now that Judah had become a Roman province, a census had to be taken because direct Roman taxation would not be imposed. There were riots and a new revolutionary movement was born (3.5). Herod had his taxes, but there was some tangible benefit for the people. Roman taxes were for Roman good, and the tax burden was certainly not going to be any less. It is evidently this census of 6 CE that is mistakenly associated with the birth of Jesus (Luke 2:1–3). Luke dated it a decade too early, but the other details fit. While Herod was a client king, the Romans did not collect taxes directly from the Jews and were unlikely to have conducted a census in Judaea during his lifetime. Writing toward the end of the first century, long after the events, Luke has apparently just got something confused.

Those who wanted direct Roman rule now got their wish – and probably lived to regret it. Roman rule was for Roman benefit. The Roman governors were often ignorant of local traditions and customs, and apparently often did not care, anyway. The ten-year governorship of Pilate (26–36 CE) was a series of clashes with the Jews over various issues; even the Roman historian Tacitus rated his administration poorly. Direct Roman rule over Judah lasted for 35 years and reminded people how much better off they had been under Herodian rule.

Herod's grandson Agrippa was well-known to the emperor's family and became a personal friend of Caligula. When Caligula was made emperor in 37 CE, Agrippa was further given the old territories of Philip (who had died). In 38 CE he was further given the tetrarchy of Antipas (who was removed from office by Caligula). He was able to intervene when in 40 CE Caligula planned to place his own statue into the Jerusalem temple. Then, with the death of Caligula, the new emperor Claudius also made him king over Judaea in 41 CE so that he now ruled over territory comparable in size to that of Herod the Great. Evidently, Agrippa I was generally well liked by his subjects, though he is presented as a persecutor of the early Christians in the book of Acts (ch. 12, where he is mistakenly called Herod). His reign was short, however; he died in 44 CE after ruling only three years over Judaea and seven years in all. Thus after a brief respite, Judaea was once again a Roman province and subject to Roman governors. For the next 20 years the country drifted toward an inevitable conflict with the ruling power.

1.1.10 *The 66–70 War with Rome and its Consequences: A New Form of Judaism*

The details of the events before and during the 66–70 will be discussed in a later chapter, where various revolutionary sects can also be brought into the picture (see 3.6). The outcome was predictable; why the Jewish leadership ever thought it could win against Rome is a puzzle, as are the many activities of the various revolutionary groups which made them fight each other more intensely than the Romans. In any case, the religious conse-quences were profound. The war and the destruction of the temple had an extremely significant influence on Judaism. Many groups seem to have been wiped out in the war; this was apparently the case with Qumran (and the Essenes as a whole?; 2.8). Also, up until 70 the chief means of worship for most Jews in Judaea and the surrounding area had been the temple cult. When there was no temple, something had to be substituted for the cult if religion was to be maintained. Those sections of Judaism which had their base in the temple dwindled in importance: the priesthood and probably the Sadducees (2.7). The groups which grew and developed were those with the potential to continue without a functioning cult. The Christians did not need a temple because they had Jesus, but in a short time they ceased to be a Jewish sect and became a separate religion. Another group which could function without a cult was the Pharisees.

The restructuring of Judaism took place at a small town near the Mediterranean coast called Yavneh (Jamnia). A leading sage named Yohanon ben Zakkai was allowed by the Romans to establish an academy or place of study of some sort. It is not even certain that he was a Pharisee, but Pharisaic views seem to have been well represented at Yavneh. Representatives from a number of groups seem to have gathered there, and it is likely that a variety of these had their input into the new synthesis which became Rabbinic Judaism. One major contribution seems to have come from Pharisaic tradition. The early strata of the Mishnah are dominated by the schools of Hillel and Shammai, as well as a few other pre-70 figures. If these were Pharisees, then Rabbinic Judaism had received a large Pharisaic content in its early stages. Yet the interests of the Pharisees appear to have been somewhat different from those of Rabbinic Judaism.

One of the main changes of emphasis had to do with Torah study as a religious activity. There is little evidence in the pre-70 rabbinic traditions that the Pharisees emphasized study as a part of their religious practice; rather the traditions focus on eating meals in – and otherwise maintaining a state of – ritual purity. Study as an act of worship became the centre of Judaism after 70. One suggestion is that this aspect of Rabbinic Judaism was the contribution of the scribes for whom the study of the written Word was central. If this interpretation is correct, Rabbinic Judaism is a synthesis of various elements of pre-70 Judaism, but two of the main contributors were the Pharisees and the scribes. However, Rabbinic Judaism was not to be identified with any particular pre-70 group; on the contrary, it was a new creation with its own identity even while borrowing various aspects of the earlier pluralistic Judaism.

1.1.11 *Further Jewish Revolts against Rome*

This new form of Judaism did not develop overnight, of course. The activities of Yavneh covered much of the period between 70 and the Bar-Kokhba Revolt. It is also evident that other ideas continued to circulate. The traditions which have come down from the Yavnean period do not have much in the way of apocalyptic or eschatological elements, yet we know that these had by no means disappeared. The *Apocalypses of 4 Ezra, 2 Baruch,* and *Abraham* all seem to date from about 100 CE. *2 Enoch* may be from about the same time. *4 Ezra* and *2 Baruch* both show the acute loss felt over the temple by many Jews and the intense questioning about God and his ways. How could God allow these things to happen to his temple? How could he allow his people to be in this situation?

There were also Jews who were not convinced that Roman rule was inevitable. Whether or not they were bolstered by apocalyptic speculations is not known, but this may have been so in some cases at least. Some Jews certainly expected Rome to fall in the near future, as the Eagle Vision shows (*4 Ezra* 11–12). Whatever the reason, a further series of revolts broke out. As it turns out the Jewish community was not yet ready to bow unconditionally to the Roman will.

During the reign of Trajan matters came to a head in several areas of the ancient Near East that were under Roman rule. A series of revolts took place in the period 115–117 CE. We have only brief information from the Roman historian Cassius Dio (68.32.1–3), and also the Christian writers Eusebius (*Hist. eccl.* 4.2.1–5) and Orosius (7.12.6–8). In addition, some papyri relating to events in Egypt are preserved from the archive of a general named Apollonius. These revolts primarily involved the Jewish communities of Egypt, Cyrenaica, Mesopotamia, and Cyprus. As far as we know, Palestine was not involved (though some have argued that it was; however, all surviving accounts are silent on this). We know little about the revolts in the various areas, but they seem to have been quite bloody on both sides, and many Jewish communities were wiped out. The beginning seems to have been in Egypt. The Jews acquitted themselves against the Roman army for a time, but in the end few seem to have survived.

For Cyrenaica we have hardly any direct information, but many buildings, especially temples, have inscriptions indicating they were rebuilt after destruction by the Jews at this time. Sources indicate the revolt was led by a 'king'. Similarly, the Jews in Cyprus was alleged to have been led by a 'king', suggesting messianic expectations in both cases. After the uprising was put down, an edict was apparently issued forbidding any Jews to settle on the island. We have no details about what happened in Mesopotamia, but it apparently related to Trajan's Parthian war. As he advanced east, the Jews seem to have revolted in the newly created Roman provinces left behind. As far as we know, these were not instigated by the Parthians but originated among the Jews themselves. The years 115–117 thus left large areas bereft of a Jewish population.

Judaea itself, however, did not have to wait too long to follow suit. Fifteen years later it began another revolt under the leadership of Simon ben Kosiba, better known as Bar Kokhba. This was in 132–135 CE. Only a few details are known of this revolt: a few brief references in the Roman writings of Cassius Dio (69.12.1–14.13) and *Historia Augusta* (*Hadrian* 5.2; 14.2) and the Christian writers Eusebius (*Hist. eccl.* 4.6.1–4) and Orosius (7.13.4–5). In the past few decades some original documents from the time of Bar Kokhba have become available, including some of his own letters. Although we cannot know the course of the war, the available sources indicate that the Romans suffered heavily, to the point that when Hadrian wrote to the Senate, he did not use the usual phrase, 'I and the legions are well'. But the Jews suffered even more greatly. This time the Romans took steps to see that there were no more Jewish insurrections. They turned Jerusalem into a Roman city called Aelia Capitolina, a pagan cult was set up on the temple site, and Jews were forbidden to enter within the walls. (For further information, see 3.7.) There was no doubt that the Jewish people were in for a long period without temple or country.

1.2 The Sources: How Do We Know What We Know?

It is very important for students to be aware of the source of our knowledge of the Jews and Judaism during this period. This survey of history given in the past few pages did not leap fully formed from the head of a university professor – like Venus from the head of Zeus. It comes from painstaking study of the few sources available to us. This work has required a great deal of patience, knowledge of languages, and careful weighing of evidence, but there is nothing mysterious about the historical method as such. On the whole, it is simply the application of many of the common-sense principles we already use in our daily lives. The sources are finite and are the basis of all studies on this period. If scholars differ, it is not usually because of using different sources but because of different interpretations and methodological approaches. This section focuses mainly on the literary sources. Some other sources (e.g. the Zenon papyri) are mentioned in later chapters. For information on the archaeology, see the information in my books listed at the end of the chapter.

1.2.1 Books of the Bible

Several books of the Bible were written during the Second Temple period and serve as useful sources for certain sorts of information. There is a considerable scholarly debate on dating and editing of the various biblical books (for a convenient discussion, see Soggin 1989).

Two biblical books claim to describe the Jews of Palestine in the Persian period; these are Ezra and Nehemiah. One of the most accepted conclusions of today is that much of the book of Nehemiah is based on Nehemiah's personal account (the so-called 'Nehemiah Memorial/Memoir'). Thus, we have some indication not only of Nehemiah's deeds but even of his attitudes and (private?) thoughts. This is valuable material; on the other hand, we must recognize that it is very one-sided and reflects the entrenched opinions and biases of a strong-willed man. We can hardly use it as a dispassionate chronicle of events. Nehemiah's own firmly held views shape the entire narrative.

The material in Ezra is quite different. In it are a number of alleged documents of the Persian administration. Although these have been widely accepted as authentic in recent English-language commentaries, their genuineness has been strongly questioned in Continental scholarship. Similarly, the Ezra story (sometimes called the 'Ezra Memoir') has been variously assessed, some seeing a good deal of history in it but others arguing that the historical Ezra is too deeply hidden to say much with any confidence. There is no agreement even on when Ezra was supposed to have lived. The end result of the debate is that the book of Nehemiah tells us something about events in Judah of his time, even if from a one-sided perspective, but the events described in Ezra are problematic.

1.2.2 Josephus

The backbone of any history of this period is the writings of Flavius Josephus (37–c. 100 CE). He is the only Jewish historian whose works are extant to any degree. Whatever his weaknesses – and there are many – we have no option because there is nothing else with such complete information. The important thing is to use his writings critically, recognizing his aims, his biases, the quality and extent of his sources, and gaps in his information. Too often passages from his works are cited without due consideration given to the normal process of historical criticism.

Josephus lived through many of the momentous events of the first century. He was sent to Galilee when the war broke out. After approximately a year there, he was besieged in the city of Jotapata and captured by Vespasian. He claims to have predicted that Vespasian would become emperor; sure enough, this happened a year or so later. At this point, Josephus was released from his bonds and became the emperor's guest instead of his prisoner. After the war he was taken to Rome, adopted into the Flavian family (hence, the name Flavius), and given a pension. Josephus' first writing was the *War* produced in the 70s. It extends from the Maccabaean revolt to the fall of Masada in 73 CE. Much of the book is given over to the events of the 66–70 war, for which Josephus drew on his own experiences and other contemporary reports. For the earlier period he depended heavily on Nicolaus of Damascus, the secretary of Herod the Great who wrote a universal history.

His next work was the *Antiquities* which begins with Creation and goes all the way up to 66 CE just before the war began. It seems to have been issued in the early 90s. The first half of the book depends on the biblical text. When the biblical material ran out, he had little information for about 200 years until he could pick up 1 Maccabees and then Nicolaus. Another work was the *Contra Apionem* (Against Apion) which was an apology on behalf of the Jews, responding in part to anti-Jewish attacks of Apion who wrote before Josephus was born. Perhaps his final work was his *Vita* (Life) which he wrote in the mid-90s in response to an attack by a fellow countryman. At this time Justus of Tiberias who had been secretary to Agrippa II evidently wrote a work which made certain accusations against Josephus. Josephus' response was an account of his activities during the revolt which by and large parallel the account already given in the *War* but with some important and interesting differences. Sadly, we do not have Justus' account which could have given us another perspective.

Apart from Josephus we have hardly any other Jewish historical writings from this time. Philo has a couple of tractates only (see next section); otherwise, we have some fragments of Jewish writers in Greek who wrote several different sorts of literature including history. Because their works are fragmentary, they do not give us a great deal, but they have a few pieces of interesting information. This includes a few quotations from Justus of Tiberias and a summary of his work.

1.2.3 Philo of Alexandria

Philo (c. 20 BCE–50 CE) is known mainly for his biblical commentaries making use of the allegorical method. He is therefore very important for the history of biblical interpretation rather than for history of the Jews. However, he was head of a delegation sent by the Jewish community to defend them before the Roman emperor against the attacks of the Greek inhabitants (38–41 CE). He wrote about the attacks on the Alexandrian Jewish community in 38, his own mission to Rome, and the plans by the emperor Caligula to place his statue in the Jerusalem temple in two tractates, *Flaccum* and *Legatio ad Gaium* (*Mission to Gaius* [*Caligula*]). These two are important historical treatises which give us a contemporary Jewish perspective on events of the time.

1.2.4 The Apocrypha

The term Apocrypha (Greek "hidden") is applied to a set of writings which are in the Catholic (Roman and Orthodox) canon but not in the Jewish or Protestant canons (the term Deutero-canonical is sometimes used of most of them): 1 Baruch, Ben Sira (Ecclesiasticus), 1 Esdras, *4 Ezra* (2 Esdras – not in the Roman canon), Judith, 1 Maccabees, 2 Maccabees, Tobit, Wisdom of Solomon, some additional sections to Daniel (Susanna and the Elders, the Song of the Three Martyrs, Bel and the Dragon). This collection is the result of historical accident. There is nothing special or mysterious about these books. They are made up of a variety of literary genres: epistle, history, tale, wisdom. They are as early as some of the books of the Hebrew Bible, and there is nothing to set them apart from the canonical books.

1.2.5 The Pseudepigrapha

The name Pseudepigrapha implies writings falsely attributed. This is not actually very helpful because scholars agree that much of the canonical literature is also pseudepigraphical. In practice, the term tends to include all early Jewish writings which are not part of the canon or of the Apocrypha. The most recent complete collection of the Pseudepigrapha has over 60 writings, though a number of these are from the second century CE or later.

The main pre-70 writings are *1 Enoch, Jubilees, Psalms of Solomon, Testament of Moses, Testament of Abraham,* and the *Letter of Aristeas.* From about the year 100 CE are *4 Ezra, 2 Baruch,* and probably the *Apocalypse of Abraham.* Some other writings are more difficult to date; for example, *2 Enoch* is currently under debate though many would put it in the late first century; the *Book of Biblical Antiquities* (*Liber Antiquitatum Biblicarum* or Pseudo-Philo) is also probably first century. Some of the material of *Sibylline Oracle* 3 is from the second century BCE, but the present form of the writing is probably from the late first century CE. *Sibylline Oracle* 4 seems to come from about 80 CE. *Sibylline Oracle* 5 is from the first half of the second century CE. There is also the literature on Adam and Eve (*Life of Adam and Eve, Apocalypse of Moses*), the *Ascension of Isaiah,* the *Testament of Job,* and the *Testament of Solomon.*

There is a strong debate over the *Testaments of the Twelve Patriarchs*; some argue they are Jewish writings which have sub-sequently been revised by Christians; others argue they are Christian writings which have made use of various Jewish tradi-tions. We know that at least two of them are pre-Christian because fragments have been found among the Qumran scrolls, though the present form of these two may be revised from the Jewish originals: *Testaments of Naphtali* and *Levi.*

1.2.6 The Dead Sea Scrolls

Since 1947 a great many writings have been found in the Judaean desert west of the Dead Sea. Many of these were found in the Qumran caves and are the specific writings known as the Qumran scrolls. The Dead Sea Scrolls also take in writings from other areas, however, including Wadi Murabba'at, Masada, the wadis Naḥal Ḥever and Naḥal Ṣe'elim; they include business docu-ments, personal legal documents such as marriage contracts, letters from the Bar Kokhba period, and biblical scrolls.

The Qumran scrolls include a variety of writings. Portions of every book of the Old Testament except Esther have been found among them. Some of the books of the Apocrypha and Pseudepigrapha are now known in a more original form from remains among the Qumran manuscripts. In addition there are many writings not hitherto known. Some of these seem to be writings taken into the Qumran library from outside, but others appear to be books written by members of the Qumran sect and are thus often referred to as 'sectarian' scrolls from Qumran. These 'sectarian' writings include the *Community Rule* or *Manual of Discipline* (1QS), the *War Scroll* (1QM), the *Thanksgiving Hymns* or *Hodayot* (1QH), and many biblical commentaries such as on Habakkuk (1QpHab), Psalm 37 (4QpPs^a), and Nahum (4QpNah). One writing already known is the *Damascus Document* (CD). This had been found in the late nineteenth century among manuscripts in an old synagogue in Cairo. It has also surfaced at Qumran, suggesting that it had been found and copied by some Jews in the Middle Ages.

Other writings may or may not have been composed by the Qumran community. For example, the *Temple Scroll* (11QT) covers many of the regulations relating to the temple cult, some of them parallel to those in Deuteronomy but others are different or new, yet scholars are divided over its provenance. A great many other previously unknown writings have been found.

1.3 Guide to Further Reading

For an introduction and survey of the debate about the history of ancient Israel, as well as of the history itself, see:

> Grabbe, Lester L. *Ancient Israel: What Do We Know and How Do We Know it?* (London/New York: T & T Clark International).

Much of the information not only in this chapter but also throughout this book is discussed at much greater length, citing primary sources and secondary studies, in my book:

> Grabbe, Lester L. *Judaism from Cyrus to Hadrian* (Minneapolis, MN: Fortress, 1992; London: SCM, 1994).

A more detailed study, aimed mainly at specialists is found in:

> Grabbe, Lester L. *A History of the Jews and Judaism in the Second Temple Period 1: Yehud: A History of the Persian*

Province of Judah (Library of Second Temple Studies 47; London/New York: T & T Clark International, 2004).

Grabbe, Lester L. *A History of the Jews and Judaism in the Second Temple Period 2: The Coming of the Greeks: The Early Hellenistic Period (335–175 BCE)* (Library of Second Temple Studies 68; London/New York: T & T Clark International, 2008).

Important specialized studies for parts of this period are:

Schürer, Emil, *The Jewish People in the Age of Jesus Christ* (revised G. Vermes, et al.; 3 vols. in 4; Edinburgh: T & T Clark, 1973–87).

Smallwood, E. M. *The Jews under Roman Rule* (SJLA 20; Leiden: Brill, 1976; corrected reprint 1981).

For a standard but easily accessible introduction to biblical literature, see:

Soggin, J. Alberto, *Introduction to the Old Testament* (3rd edn; London: SCM, 1989).

An English translation of Josephus can be found in:

Thackeray, H. St. J., et al. *Josephus* (Loeb Classical Library; London: Heineman; Cambridge: Harvard, 1926–65).

An older translation of Josephus from 1737 has been reprinted many times, most recently:

The Works of Josephus: New Updated Edition (translator W. Whiston; Peabody, MA: Hendrickson, 1987).

English translations of Philo are provided by:

The Works of Philo: New Updated Edition. Complete and Unabridged (translator C. D. Yonge; updated with foreword by David M. Scholer; Peabody, MA: Hendrickson, 1993).

Colson, F. H., and G. H. Whitaker. *Philo* (vols. 1–10; Loeb Classical Library; Cambridge, MA: Harvard; London: Heinemann, 1929–43).

For a survey of the main Jewish writings during the Second Temple period, see:

Nickelsburg, George W. E. *Jewish Literature between the Bible and the Mishnah* (Minneapolis, MN: Fortress, 2nd edn, 2005).

Stone, Michael E. (ed.) *Jewish Writings of the Second Temple Period* (Compendia rerum iudaicarum ad Novum Testamentum 2/2; Minneapolis, MN: Fortress; 1984).

For Jewish literature composed in Greek, a good introduction is:

Collins, John J. *Between Athens and Jerusalem: Jewish Identity in the Hellenistic Diaspora* (The Biblical Resource Series; Grand Rapids, MI: Eerdmans; Livonia, MI: Dove Booksellers, 2nd edn, 2000).

Translations of the Jewish writings in the Apocrypha are found in many editions of the Bible, such as the Revised Standard Version, New Revised Standard Version, New English Bible, Revised English Bible. The most complete collection of the Pseudepigrapha is:

Charlesworth, J. H. (ed.) *Old Testament Pseudepigrapha* (2 vols; Garden City, NY: Doubleday, 1983–85).

Less comprehensive but useful is:

Sparks, H. (ed.) *The Apocryphal Old Testament* (Oxford: Clarendon, 1984),

but despite its name, it does not have the Apocrypha in it, only some of the major Pseudepigrapha. An older collection of the Apocrypha and some of the Pseudepigrapha is still very useful, not least because of the commentaries, even if now rather out of date:

> Charles, R. H. (ed.) *Apocrypha and Pseudepigrapha of the Old Testament* (2 vols; Oxford: Clarendon, 1913).

For the Jewish historians other than Josephus and preserved only in fragments, a translation is given in Charlesworth (ed.), *Old Testament Pseudepigrapha*, vol. 2, pp. 775–919. An edition, with translation and commentary, is given in:

> Holladay, Carl R. *Fragments from Hellenistic Jewish Authors, Volume I: Historians* (Texts and Translations 20, Pseudepigrapha Series 10; Atlanta: Scholars, 1983); *Volume II: Poets: The Epic Poets Theodotus and Philo and Ezekiel the Tragedian* (Texts and Translations 30, Pseudepigrapha Series 12; Atlanta: Scholars, 1989); *Volume III: Aristobulus* (SBLTT 39, Pseudepigrapha Series 13; Atlanta: Scholars, 1995); *Volume IV: Orphica* (SBLTT 40; Pseudepigrapha Series 14; Atlanta: Scholars, 1996).

For all things relating to Qumran and the Dead Sea Scrolls, see:

> Lawrence H. Schiffman and James C. VanderKam (eds), *Encyclopaedia of the Dead Sea Scrolls* (Oxford University Press, 2000).

A collection of the main sectarian and some other writings from Qumran in English translation can be found in:

> Vermes, Geza. *The Dead Sea Scrolls in English* (4th edn; London: Penguin, 1995).

The text and an English translation of all the non-biblical Scrolls is given by:

> García Martínez, Florentino, and Eibert J. C. Tigchelaar (eds and transl.). 1997–98. *The Dead Sea Scrolls Study*

Edition: Volume One 1Q1–4Q273; Volume Two 4Q274–11Q31 (Leiden: Brill).

Good introductions to the archaeology and general scholarship on the Qumran community are:

Davies, Philip R. *Qumran* (Cities of the Biblical World; Guildford, Surrey: Lutterworth, 1982).

Magness, Jodi, *The Archaeology of Qumran and the Dead Sea Scrolls* (Studies in the Dead Sea Scrolls and Related Literature; Grand Rapids, MI: Eerdmans, 2002).

Papyri relating to the Jews of Egypt, including some referring to the 115–117 revolt, can be found in:

Tcherikover, V. A., A. Fuks, and M. Stern, *Corpus Papyrorum Judaicarum* (3 vols; Cambridge, MA: Harvard; Jerusalem: Magnes, 1957–64).

CHAPTER 2

⋘∞⋙

TEXTUAL JUDAISM: THE PRIESTLY AND SCRIBAL CURRENT

2.1 Introduction

It is natural that people often assume that Judaism in the Second Temple period was more or less like contemporary Judaism, in which people meet weekly or even more frequently in synagogues to pray, worship, and hear the Bible read. The written scripture and its reading and study are assumed to be the focus of Judaism at all times. There is no question that the written law, especially the Pentateuch (Torah), has been very important to Judaism at least from Ptolemaic times. For example, it seems likely that the Pentateuch was translated into Greek about the middle of the third century BCE for the benefit of the Alexandrian and other Diaspora communities whose first language was Greek.

Yet the Judaism of pre-70 times was formally structured in a quite different way from the Judaism of later times. The main religious institution was the Jerusalem temple, and temple worship went back many centuries in Jewish and Israelite history. The temple was not the same as a synagogue. The main activity in the temple was blood sacrifice. There were required sacrifices on a daily, weekly, and monthly basis and also at the major religious festivals. If an individual committed a trespass of the law, a sacrifice was required. If one wanted to thank God for blessings, particular sacrifices could be given. Thus, Jewish men were expected to come up on a regular basis to worship at the temple and participate in the cult; the sources suggest that many and perhaps even most male Jews in Palestine came up one or more times a year to the temple.

The emphasis on blood sacrifice should not be misconstrued, as abhorrent as the practice may seem to some. It was not 'empty ritual' as so often portrayed in prejudiced Christian (usually Protestant) propaganda. On the contrary, the sacrificial ritual was suffused with deep religious symbolism. This symbolism was taken up into later Judaism, after the cessation of the temple cult, and into Christianity. The central Christian metaphor is, after all, the *sacrifice* of Christ – which has little meaning if the Israelite sacrificial system is not taken into account. Temple worship was also often a social and family occasion, because the bulk of most sacrificial animals went to the offerer, with only certain portions being burned on the altar or going to the priest. The rest of the meat was consumed by the one offering the sacrifice, along with the family and friends.

Also, there was more to the temple as an institution than just the sacrificial cult, important as that was. The priests were the custodians of the law (see section 2.2 below) and were responsible for teaching it to the people. How they did this is not clear in our extant sources. There may have been public readings of the law. It is possible that there were public expositions. The temple also served as a place of prayer. Singing and other liturgical recitations were also a part of the temple service, though it is not clear how they fitted in with the sacrificial ritual. All in all, the temple was a worship centre for Palestinian Jews with many different opportunities for the individual to participate.

What of synagogues? They are not attested until the third century BCE and then first in the Diaspora in Egypt and Asia Minor. That is, they seem to have developed in areas where Jews did not have access to the temple. Prior to their growth, Jews seem to have conducted prayers and worship in the home (cf. Tobit 2:1–2; 3:10–16; Daniel 6:10). Most Jews in Palestine were not so far away from the temple that they could not go to it on a regular basis for worship. For this reason, there seems to have been no pressing need for any other place of worship. Thus, the synagogue does not seem to have been introduced into Palestine until quite late, perhaps in the first century BCE. Few synagogues are attested in pre-70 sources, and few if any pre-70 remains have been found by archaeologists. The synagogue seems to have become important to Palestinian Jews only at a late time, perhaps in the last decades while the Second Temple stood.

Nevertheless, it is clear that many Jews had access to the Torah in one form or another. Writings from many different quarters show a knowledge of the law and an intense interest in understanding and interpreting it. The same applies to the prophetic writings and other books in our present Hebrew Bible or Old Testament. When and how the present canon became finalized is still not known, despite a number of studies on the subject. Some Jewish groups seem to have accepted a different set of books as authoritative compared to other groups. For example, *1 Enoch* seems to have been part of the canon of some groups (cf. Jude 14; the *Testament of Levi* 14:1; the Ethiopic church). But most Jews seem to have accepted the Torah and most of the prophetic books by the first century CE. Therefore, the written Word and its interpretation were very important to Judaism even while the temple stood. Many different groups appealed to the Word and thus made up the current we can designate as 'textual Judaism'.

2.2 Priests and Levites

The priesthood in general, and the high priest in particular, dominated the Jewish state during the Second Temple period. As might be expected, the priests were in charge of the temple and the operation of the cult. They were also responsible for the governance of Judaea as a political entity in the larger Near Eastern empire – first the Persian, then the Ptolemaic, followed by the Seleucid. They headed the independent Hasmonean Jewish state, when the rule became that of priest-kings. Under the Romans, the priests had to relinquish much of their political power to the Herodians under Herod the Great, his son Archelaus, Agrippa I, and even to some extent with regard to Agrippa II. Yet they maintained control of the temple and were still the most important figures of the religious establishment.

What is not often realized is the extent to which the priests – the altar priests and the Levites – were also the transmitters of the written scriptures, the cultivators of wisdom, the interpreters of the religious tradition, and even the authors and editors of the written Word. The importance of the priests has often been overlooked and the study of their activities neglected in favour of apocalyptic groups, sects such as the Pharisees, and revolutionaries. Yet priests could be members of all these groups, as well as dynamic contributors to all aspects of Jewish religious life.

The priests were first and foremost cult functionaries. They had the responsibility to carry out the sacrificial system which lay at the heart of Israelite religion. This is their main function as indicated in the book of Leviticus which gives detailed information on the sacrificial cult and the functioning of the priesthood. They continued to have this important task until the temple was finally destroyed in 70 CE. To make sure that they could devote themselves to their cultic duties, they had been assigned the tithes of agricultural produce, other offerings such as first fruits, and a portion of each sacrifice offered (except for the whole burnt offering).

Yet once the cult was centralized in Jerusalem there were more priests available for service at the altar than were needed most of the time. According to later sources, the priests were eventually divided into 24 courses, each one serving two weeks during the year plus all being available at major festival times. Even before this division, however, the priests would have been the one portion of the Israelite population (apart from the few very wealthy) who had the leisure necessary to pursue intellectual activities to any great extent. This is a very important fact to be aware of. The average Israelite worked from dawn to dusk to make a bare living, much as peasants still do the world over. The reduction in workload created by mechanization is a recent phenomenon. The average Israelite or Jew of antiquity did not normally have opportunities for education or ready access to books and literature. The educated lay person seldom existed.

This needs to be recognized. The image of the priest as merely a cultic official with no interests or duties outside this is widespread but mistaken. (Indeed, there is a strong anti-clerical bias in some religious circles and even in scholarship itself.) Thus, theological innovation, the cultivation of wisdom, the development of ethical thought, and the careful attention to daily religious duties are all often ascribed to non-priests. Modern writers frequently talk of deuteronomists, sages, prophets, apocalypticists, Pharisees, and scribes, carelessly overlooking the fact that priests might well be any of these. Being a priest on duty at the altar did not prevent one from systematizing traditional wisdom, engaging in cosmic and even apocalyptic speculation, reflecting on the theological significance of the religious rites and traditions, or developing ideas about the right way to live in relationship to God and other human beings. On the contrary, it was likely to be the priests who had the education, the leisure, the intellectual stimulus, and the interest to do such things.

The priesthood was far broader than just the 'sons of Aaron', however; it included the 'lower clergy' known by the name of Levites. These had the care of the fabric of the buildings, security, cleaning, provisioning, and other support for the priests who actually presided at the altar. While some of these activities may have been menial, others implied a considerable degree of responsibility. In addition, some of the Levites seem to have carried out the many scribal activities necessary for the maintenance and smooth operation of the temple.

The late books of the Old Testament, such as Ezra, Nehemiah, and Chronicles, show a number of offices among the Levites and other clergy. Within Ezra and Nehemiah the division between the priests and Levites is assumed. The genealogies in Ezra 2 and Nehemiah 7 break down the various cultic personnel into Levites, singers, gatekeepers, temple servants, and priests (Ezra 2:36–63; Nehemiah 7:39–60,72). The priestly oracle of the Urim and Thummim had apparently ceased to exist (Ezra 2:63). The books of 1 and 2 Chronicles give one of the most complete descriptions of the organization of the priesthood, especially 1 Chronicles 23–26. They picture David as having brought the priesthood into order in preparation for Solomon to build the temple, but other passages such as 2 Chronicles 5 and 7 also refer to celebrations in the temple. Of particular interest are the references to singing and music which have little place in the Pentateuch or the Deuteronomistic History (Joshua – 2 Kings). The books of Chronicles are also associated with prophecy, suggesting a connection between the Levites and cult prophecy (1 Chronicles 25; 2 Chronicles 20:14–17).

The books of Chronicles emphasize the judging and teaching functions of the priests. It is stated in 2 Chronicles 15:3 that, during the reign of Asa, Israel had gone many days without the true God and without a priest to teach (*mōreh*) and without teaching (*tôrāh*). According to 2 Chronicles 19:5–11, Jehoshaphat appointed Levites and priests among the judges in Judah. The high priest Amariah was to be in overall charge of judgements relating to God, with the Levite officers to assist (2 Chronicles 19:11; cf. 1 Chronicles 23:4). Levites also filled the office of scribe (2 Chronicles 34:13; cf. 1 Chronicles 26:29). Although these passages are supposedly describing the priesthood under the Israelite monarchy, it has long been argued that the situation actually being sketched is that of the Second Temple period. If so, this may provide a picture of the temple organization in the late Persian or the early Greek period.

The temple singers come up again some centuries later, in the decade before the destruction of the Second Temple. At this time, the temple singers appealed to king Agrippa II to wear special white linen garments which had evidently been hitherto reserved for the priesthood (*Antiquities* 20.9.6 §§216–18). Although Agrippa was king of the old tetrarchy of Philip (Trachonitis, Batanaea, Gaulanitis) and not Judaea (which was now a Roman province with a Roman governor), he nevertheless had certain privileges with regard to the Jerusalem temple. He ruled in favour of the singers, and they were able to wear the coveted garments for the few years remaining of the temple's existence.

In the Second Temple period, there is evidence that the priests were the ones who interpreted and provided authoritative rulings about the law. According to Haggai, the prophet was sent to the priests to obtain a legal interpretation (2:10–13). Some centuries later Josephus tells how the temple manager stopped the sacrifices for the Roman emperor. As a result the priests were called upon to decide the religious issue in the light of legal interpretations of the Torah (*War* 2.17.2–4 §§409–17; *Against*

Apion 2.21–22 §§184–88; *Life 39* §§196–98). Although there may have been legal experts who were laymen, the priesthood was still accepted as the custodians and interpreters of the law.

2.3 Priestly Rule of Judah

Whatever its activities outside the strict boundaries of the cult during the monarchy, the priesthood took on an important new role during the post-exilic period. Despite evidence of hopes among many Jews, the Davidic dynasty had not been restored. Some have suggested that Zerubbabel had pretentions to the throne and was subsequently removed from office by the Persians, but the arguments for this are not particularly strong. Yet however much some Jews may have longed for a return to kingly rule, it was not to be at this time. Judah was a Persian province with a Persian governor, even if that governor was himself Jewish at least some of the time.

Whether or not there was a provincial governor during the Persian and Greek periods, various sources show the importance of the high priest in the internal Jewish government. In some cases, the high priest may have been the official governor; at other times, the ruling power looked to the high priest as the main representative of the Jewish people. Whether officially or unofficially the high priest appears to have been the *de facto* head of the native administration. There are also indications that others of the priesthood assisted him in this task. An early description of the rule by priests is found in the account of Hecateus of Abdera, writing towards the beginning of Greek rule (c.300 BCE). His writing is quoted by the Greek historian Diodorus Siculus (40.3.1–7):

> [4] . . . He [Moses] picked out the men of most refinement and with the greatest ability to head the entire nation, and appointed them priests; and he ordained that they should occupy themselves with the temple and the honours and sacrifices offered to their God. [5] These same men he appointed to be judges in all major disputes, and entrusted to them the guardianship of the laws and customs. For this reason the Jews never have a king, and authority over the people is regularly vested in whichever priest is regarded as

superior to his colleagues in wisdom and virtue. They call this man the high priest, and believe that he acts as a messenger to them of god's commandments. [6] It is he, we are told, who in their assemblies and other gatherings announces what is ordained, and the Jews are so docile in such matters that straightway they fall to the ground and do reverence to the high priest when he expounds the commandments to them . . . [7] He [Moses] led out military expeditions against the neighbouring tribes, and after annexing much land apportioned it out, assigning equal allotments to private citizens and greater ones to the priests, in order that they, by virtue of receiving more ample revenues, might be undistracted and apply themselves continually to the worship of God.

The place of the high priest in the structure of government is made apparent in the semi-legendary account of the Tobiads under Ptolemaic rule during the third century BCE. As already described (1.1.3), the high priest Onias II was responsible for paying the tribute due to the Ptolemaic rulers. Half a century later Simon II, who was high priest at the time that the Seleucids took Palestine, had not only cultic but also civic obligations (Ben Sira 50:1–5):

The leader of his brothers and the pride of his people was the high priest, Simon son of Onias, who in his life repaired the house, and in his time fortified the temple. He laid the foundations for the high double walls, the high retaining walls for the temple enclosure. In his days a water cistern was dug, a reservoir like the sea in circumference. He considered how to save his people from ruin, and fortified the city against siege. How glorious he was, surrounded by the people, as he came out of the house of the curtain.

The importance of the high priest has already been well indicated by the events of the 'Hellenistic reform' (see section 1.1.4) and the Maccabaean revolt (1.1.5). The Maccabaean successes only increased the importance of the high priest, and the Hasmonaeans became priest-kings. The zenith of high priestly power was thus reached during the period of Hasmonaean rule. When the Hasmonaean kingdom was ended by the Romans, the position of the high priest as nominal head of the Jews continued, though his position had reverted to something similar to that under previous overlords. Once Herod had become king, he took away any independent authority of the high priest, though the latter was still the chief cultic official. Herod appointed and deposed the high priest at will. After his death, when Judaea became a Roman province, the prestige of the office began to revive to some extent; however, the Romans retained the right to appoint and depose the high priest. When Agrippa I became king, he took over the rights of his grandfather Herod the Great. Then, at the end of his short reign, these rights with regard to the priesthood eventually passed to his son Agrippa II even though the latter was not king of Judaea.

2.4 The Wise and the Intellectual Tradition

The wisdom books take up a significant section of the Old Testament: Proverbs, Job, and Qohelet (Ecclesiastes), plus the deutero-canonical books of Ben Sira and Wisdom of Solomon. At one time, the wisdom literature was neglected and down-played in theological study. In recent years, however, a great deal of scholarly interest has centred on these books and a more balanced view generally prevails. Although one can still occasionally read statements to the effect that the wisdom books represent 'an alien body' in the Old Testament, more frequent are those that place wisdom at the centre of Old Testament theology. At the very least, the importance of wisdom for Old Testament literature and theology is now widely recognized.

The most frequent word associated with wisdom in the Hebrew Bible is *ḥokmāh*. This word has a wide meaning, much as the English word 'wise' does, and can include the connotation of intellect, learning by study, practical wisdom, common sense, or other variations on the theme. Yet it is most frequently associated with the intellectual type of wisdom associated with study and formal education. Similarly, while 'the wise man/woman' can be anyone with a variety of attributes of knowledge or mental skills, the term is most often applied to those who bear the intellectual tradition. Those who can read and write, who have engaged in study, and who know literature are the wise *par excellence*.

It has not often been considered who might be those who carried on this intellectual tradition, partly because it has too frequently been assumed that formal education was widespread in Israel. Although the subject is currently under debate, there is little evidence for widespread literacy – much less for universal schooling. Recent studies have suggested that Jerusalem did not become a major centre in which an educated scribal class was needed until relatively late – in the late eighth century BCE. Only the very few had the resources and leisure for education; the vast majority of the population were peasant farmers or agricultural workers of some sort. Those able to devote time to literature were, first, the priests and Levites, and secondly, the aristocracy. This situation does not seem to have changed through the next several centuries, though we do find evidence of lay movements which attempted to master sufficient knowledge to engage in legal discussion and biblical interpretation.

2.5 Scribes

The term 'scribe' (*grammateus* in the Greek sources) has a wide meaning, similar to our word 'secretary'. It can mean the lowly scribe in a warehouse who keeps simple records and perhaps needs little more education than to be able to read and write and do certain sums; or it can refer to a high official in the government (like the 'secretary of state' in many national governments). Scribes would have functioned at various levels in Jewish society, from private (wealthy) households and businesses to civil administration to the temple itself.

Evidence for the temple scribes is found in the decree of Antiochus III quoted in Josephus (*Antiquities* 12.3.3–4 §§138–46). At the time of the conquest of Palestine by the Seleucids, Jews were apparently to be found on both sides of the conflict, some being pro-Seleucid and some pro-Ptolemaic. The pro-Seleucid group got the upper hand and opened the gates of Jerusalem to Antiochus' soldiers. As result of their support, Antiochus issued a decree permitting the free exercise of their religion and also granting certain temporary exemptions from taxation to help repair the damage done by fighting in Jerusalem:

> King Antiochus to Ptolemy, greeting. Inasmuch as the Jews, from the very moment when we entered their country, showed their eagerness to serve us and, when we came to their city, gave us

a splendid reception and met us with their senate and furnished an abundance of provisions to our soldiers and elephants, and also helped us to expel the Egyptian garrison in the citadel, we have seen fit on our part to requite them for these acts and to restore their city which has been destroyed by the hazards of war, and to repeople it by bringing back to it those who have been dispersed abroad . . . And it is my will that these things be made over to them as I have ordered, and that the work on the temple be completed, including the porticos and any other part that it may be necessary to build . . . And all the members of the nation shall have a form of government in accordance with the laws of their country, and the senate, the priests, the scribes of the temple and the temple-singers shall be relieved from the poll-tax and the crown-tax and the salt-tax which they pay. And, in order that the city may the more quickly be inhabited, I grant both to the present inhabitants and to those who may return before the month of Hyperberetaios exemption from taxes for three years.

Probably the most famous passage about scribes is found in Ben Sira, writing in the early second century (Ben Sira 38:24–39:11, New English Bible):

A scholar's wisdom comes of ample leisure; if a man is to be wise he must be relieved of other tasks. How can a man become wise who guides the plough . . . and talks only about cattle? . . . How different it is with the man who devotes himself to studying the law of the Most High, who investigates all the wisdom of the past, and spends his time studying the prophecies! He preserves the sayings of famous men and penetrates the intricacies of parables. He investigates the hidden meaning of proverbs and knows his way among riddles. The great avail themselves of his services, and he is seen in the presence of rulers. He travels in foreign countries and learns at first hand the good or evil of man's lot. He makes a point of rising early to pray . . . If it is the will of the great Lord, he will be filled with a spirit of intelligence; then he will pour forth wise sayings of his own and give thanks to the Lord in prayer. He will have sound advice and knowledge to offer, and his thoughts will dwell on the mysteries he has studied. He will disclose what he has learnt from his own education, and will take pride in the law of the Lord's covenant. Many will praise his intelligence; it will never sink into oblivion. The memory of him will not die but will live on from generation to generation;

the nations will talk of his wisdom, and his praises will be sung in the assembly. If he lives long, he will leave a name in a thousand, and if he goes to his rest, his reputation is secure.

Ben Sira makes a certain connection between being a scribe and knowing the law of God. This may be an idealized picture, representing Ben Sira's own perspective, but there seems be some truth to it. The question is, does this apply to all scribes, to some scribes, or perhaps just to the scribes associated with the temple? Ben Sira himself does not limit it to temple scribes; on the other hand, good arguments have been made to the effect that if Ben Sira was not himself a priest, he had close links with the priesthood. He associates the law with the priesthood, but it is likely that some priests had greater training and insight than others. Thus, it is not clear that Ben Sira was claiming the study of the law for every scribe at every level of society.

One of the complications of trying to understand scribes is the picture of the NT. It seems to make being a scribe into a religious office. There is little evidence in other sources that there was such a thing. However, it may be that those who were scribes by profession had special training in traditional laws as well. Indeed, it has recently been argued that the scribes of the NT are actually the Levites, trained in the law. If so, this could explain the apparent official teaching function of the scribes and also why the priests are so often absent from the Gospel tradition (i.e. they are represented by the 'scribes').

2.6 The Pharisees

Perhaps more has been written on the Pharisees than any other ancient Jewish group. There are two reasons for this: first, they have often been seen by Jewish scholars as forerunners of Rabbinic Judaism; second, their frequent mention in the NT has made them a byword in many Christian writings. Neither approach is helpful because both represent a rather biased point of view. Our task is to attempt to disentangle the Pharisees from the various sources. What soon becomes clear is how difficult the task is and how little we know for certain about them.

2.6.1 The New Testament

The Pharisees are most familiar from the pages of the Gospels. Here they appear as opponents of Jesus and are criticized as excessively concerned about legal technicalities and picayune points of the ritual law (Matthew 23:23–28; Luke 11:37–44); they are especially labelled as hypocrites who want to be admired by others but who do not take on the burden of the law which they bind on their fellow Jews (Matthew 23:4). Much of the time they, along with the other groups, are simply a foil for Jesus – a chance for him to score points at their expense and give clever replies to leading questions. Thus, we cannot necessarily assume that every confrontation with Jesus really tells us anything about the ancient Pharisees.

Yet despite its bias, the contribution of the NT is significant in two major ways: (1) it has the only writings by someone who claimed to be a Pharisee: the apostle Paul; (2) the areas indicated by the Gospels to be of interest to the Pharisees are eating, tithing, festivals, agricultural regulations, purity, and marriage – areas which coincide with the interests indicated in the early rabbinic traditions (see section 2.6.2). When we put all the passages together, the following characteristics emerge from the NT writings:

1   They have 'traditions from the fathers/elders' which are not part of the written law (Mark 7:5; Matthew 15:2; Galatians 1:14).
2   They are especially concerned with the legal minutiae of obedience, including tithing, eating of food, Sabbath observance, and the like (cf. Matthew 12:1–14; 23).
3   Some passages have them also being concerned about how to recognize the Messiah (Mark 12:35–37) and about Roman authority (Mark 12:13–17).

2.6.2 Rabbinic Literature

We would expect Jewish literature to give us the most information about the Pharisees. Appeal has often been made to rabbinic literature. Indeed, many treatments of the Pharisees have simply taken rabbinic literature as literature of the Pharisees. We have essentially three problems: (a) only a few passages refer to the *perushim,* a word usually taken to be the Hebrew origin of the term 'Pharisees' which comes from Greek literature; (b) we have no evidence that most of the rabbis before 70 CE were Pharisees or that the bulk of rabbinic literature was written by Pharisees; (c) much of the literature is centuries after 70 CE and is unlikely to have been written by Pharisees even if the latter continued to exist after 70.

On the other hand, two figures labelled as Pharisees in non-rabbinic sources seem to fit well with the other 'sages' mentioned in the Mishnah and the other early rabbinic literature (Gamaliel/Gamliel I and his son Simon/Simeon). Also the main themes of the Mishnah are ritual purity, eating, festivals, agricultural regulations, and laws relating to the exchange of women (betrothal, marriage, divorce). These are also the themes found in the early traditions about the pre-70 sages. Furthermore, they tend to have a good deal in common with the brief references in the Gospels. Scholars have felt instinctively that there must be a connection between the Pharisees and the rabbinic literature. Proving it is another matter – instinct can be very subjective and very misleading.

Even if the Pharisaic movement was taken up wholesale into rabbinic Judaism, this does not mean that rabbinic Judaism necessarily represents its outlook, emphases, and content – all of which could have been extensively altered in the transition to rabbinic Judaism. There is no question that the Mishnah, Tosefta, and other early rabbinic literature are post-70 and picture a situation in which there is no longer a functioning temple. Some of their contents may represent the pre-70 situation; on the other hand, since a good deal of these writings is plainly from a later time, trying to sort out the earlier from the later is not an easy task.

2.6.3 Josephus

The value of Josephus has already been discussed in 1.2.2. As one who reached maturity before 70, he of all sources should have knowledge of the Jewish groups extant at the time. Furthermore, he claims to have made a trial of the various sects (*Life* 2§§10–12):

> At about the age of sixteen I determined to gain personal experience of the several sects into which our nation is divided. These, as I have frequently mentioned, are three in number – the first that of the Pharisees, the second that of the Sadducees, and the third that of the Essenes. I thought that, after a thorough investigation, I should be in a position to select the best. So I submitted myself to hard training and laborious exercises and passed through the three courses . . . Being now in my nineteenth year I began to govern my life by the rules of the Pharisees, a sect having points of resemblance to that which the Greeks call the Stoic school.

This passage has in the past usually been taken to mean that Josephus embraced the Pharisees at this time in his life. A recent book has questioned this. I find it difficult to read the passage any other way than that Josephus *claims* that he became a Pharisee at this time, but it also seems clear that the rest of Josephus' writings show no evidence that he had become a Pharisee in early life. It would have been easy to make such a claim in Rome in late life when there were few around to contradict him, if he found it useful.

In any case, Josephus is an important source on the Pharisees. Yet he actually gives us very little information on them in the two main passages where he describes them (*War* 2.8.14 §§162–63, 166; *Antiquities* 18.1.2–4 §§11–15, 17):

> [T]he Pharisees, who are considered the most accurate interpreters of the laws, and hold the position of the leading sect, attribute everything to Fate and to God; they hold that to act rightly or otherwise rests, indeed, for the most part with men, but that in each action Fate co-operates. Every soul, they maintain, is imperishable, but the soul of the good alone passes into another body, while the souls of the wicked suffer eternal punishment . . . The Pharisees are affectionate to each other and cultivate harmonious relations with the community. (*War* 2.8.14 §§162–63, 166)

Yet there are other passages where Josephus talks of Pharisaic actions and individuals designated as Pharisees: *War* 1.5.2–3 §§110–14; 1.29.2 §571; 2.17.2–3 §§410–11; *Antiquities* 13.10.5–7

§§288–99; 13.15.5–16.6 §§398–432; 15.1.1 §§3–4; 15.10.4 §370; 17.2.4–3.1 §§41–47; *Life* 38 §§190–91. These give us some further information, all of which can be summarized:

1   One consistent theme is that they had a reputation for interpretation of the traditional laws not found in the books of Moses. Unfortunately, Josephus does not go on to tell us what were these laws and traditions unique to the Pharisees.

2   In a number of episodes, they appear as a group seeking political power. Only once is there evidence that they were actually able to enforce their own particular laws (whatever these were) on the people and even the priests in the temple, and this was under Alexandra Salome (76–67 BCE) when they became *de facto* rulers of state, if Josephus is to be believed. It is important to be aware of what Josephus' own account indicates, because in one passage (*Antiquities* 18.1.2–4 §§11–15, 17) he implies that their traditions were always enforced on the priests and even the Jewish rulers. This statement is not borne out by his own data *except* during Alexandra's reign. He gives no indication that they controlled either the religious or political establishment on a regular basis. On the contrary, in various passages he makes it clear that the priests control worship and the teaching of the law.

3   They believe in the soul and its reward and punishment after death, and they believe in both fate and free will. Neither of these topics is likely to have been too important to them, so this information only serves to demonstrate how little Josephus actually tells us about them. Huge questions about their beliefs, aims, lifestyle, and history remain undiscussed by him, much to our frustration.

2.6.4 *Conclusions*

I have devoted more space to the Pharisees than to any other group within this book, yet I have hardly scratched the surface of the historical and methodological problems in trying to understand them and reconstruct the historical picture. What I hope is clear is that (a) a great deal of emotional baggage has got carried along with the debate so that issues of religious belief and identity important to the researchers have become entangled with the historical question, and (b) the subject purely as a historical problem is fraught with difficulties. It is extremely important to realize how little we know about this group which has been so central to many discussions and reconstructions of Jewish religion at this time. The following tentative points can be put forward with a good deal of caution:

1   The Pharisees claimed to have traditions from the fathers which were not written in the Hebrew Bible. There is no evidence that they claimed this was 'oral law' (though the rabbis did later develop such a view); it may well have been passed down in written form. Nor is there evidence that they had the concept of a 'dual torah' – two laws given on Sinai, one written down and one passed down orally (the doctrine of the Dual Torah became central to rabbinic Judaism).

2   The best estimate about the content of these traditions is that they represented an attempt by a group trying to reproduce the temple cult in their own home. That is, the laws seemed to turn primarily on eating ordinary food in a state of cultic purity (normally required in the temple but not necessarily in the home) and thus involved questions of ritual purity, eating, tithing (since only properly tithed food could be eaten), the Sabbath, and festivals. Some laws also involved the 'exchange of women': betrothal, marriage, and divorce. These all suggest a 'table fellowship' sect. This fits with a lay movement attempting to imitate the priests, but it could equally apply to a priestly group trying to extend the temple regulations outside the temple to their own homes.

3   There is little evidence that this group dominated either religious or civil life through most of their history. What we can deduce about their laws does not suggest they were in charge of the temple (few of the regulations affect the temple cult as such) or society (there are few civil laws).

On the other hand, there is an indication that they were often trying to gain political influence but not succeeding. The one major exception is under Alexandra Salome when for a period of almost a decade they do seem to have controlled the state. If so, during that brief period they no doubt were able to enforce their views (whatever these were) to some extent on the temple cult.

2.7 The Sadducees

The Sadducees have been everyone's whipping boy. No Jewish group today claims to be heirs of the Sadducees. (There are a number of interesting parallels between them and the Qaraites, a mediaeval 'back-to-the-Bible' movement which arose in reaction to rabbinic Judaism. Whether there was any organic connection is very debatable.) There is also the possible connection between the priesthood and the Sadducees, and the Protestant prejudice against priests gets transferred to the Sadducees.

As with the Pharisees, our information about the Sadducees is very skimpy, indeed more so. There are a few passing statements in the NT (generally hostile), as well as a few brief references in Josephus (also not usually complimentary), and in a few rabbinic passages a group called the *Ṣadduqîm* are found in debate with the *Pĕrušîm* (Pharisees? – see section 2.6.2). The *Perushim* are also found in debate with a group called the Boethusians (*Baitôsîm*), who have also often been identified or associated with the Sadducees. At best, the information is very meagre, and most of the sources are hostile. This means that any historical reconstruction must be considered very uncertain. Putting together the information yields the following brief characteristics of the Sadducees, but these are even more uncertain than with the Pharisees:

1   They accept only written scripture, rejecting the 'traditions of the fathers'. This does not mean, of course, that they may not have their own traditional interpretation of the biblical text. People have always had trouble distinguishing

between what the text actually says and their interpretation of it.

2 They are said not to believe in the resurrection or angels. This is a bit of a puzzle since both are found in some books of the OT. It may be that their canon did not have all the books of the present Hebrew Bible (canonization seems to have been a long process); on the other hand, they may have rejected some traditional interpretations which involved an elaborate angelology (such as we find in 1 Enoch) or detailed speculations about the eschaton.

3 The names of both the Sadducees and Boethusians suggest a connection with the priesthood. Although the exact origin of the name Sadducees is never discussed in ancient sources, it has often been connected with Zadok, the high priest under David. The family of Zadok is given prominence in the book of Ezekiel, and after that the priests often emphasized their identification as descendents of Zadok ('sons of Zadok'). The priests in the Qumran texts are also referred to as 'sons of Zadok'. The origin of the name Boethusians is also uncertain, but it has long been connected with Boethus. This was the name of a priestly family which supplied a number of the high priests in the first centuries BCE and CE. This also suggests some sort of priestly connection, as with the Sadducees. The book of Acts also associates the Sadducees with the high priest (4:1; 5:17).

4 Josephus tells us that 'there are but few men to whom this doctrine has been made known, but these are men of the highest standing' (*Antiquities* 18.1.4 §17). Only two Sadducees are named elsewhere in his writings, but one of these is a high priest and the other is a Hasmonaean priest-king. This might suggest that the Sadducees were mainly from the upper socio-economic classes. Other sources do not claim this as such, but the high priestly family was certainly of this stratum. On the other hand, we cannot assume that all Sadducees were either wealthy or associated with the priesthood.

Much of what I have given so far is not particularly controversial. In recent years, however, a major new thesis has been
developed about the Sadducees. This identifies them with the
Qumran community. The main points of this argument are the
following: (a) the 'sons of Zadok' are important in the Qumran
documents (see section 2.8 below), and (b) the ritual practices
in the Qumran documents correspond with those espoused by
the 'Sadducees' in rabbinic literature. This is a matter which
deserves debate, especially in the light of how uncertain our
knowledge is, but it would be fair to say that scholarship has not
yet responded with enthusiasm to this suggestion.

2.8 The Essenes

Another group credited with a great emphasis on interpreting
scripture was the Essenes. These have also been widely associated with Qumran since the discovery of the Dead Sea Scrolls.
In spite of the attempt to make the Qumran group Sadducees
(see section 2.7 above), the Essene identification is still probably the prevalent theory among scholars. No other group is
better described in the early sources than the Essenes. Of the
four main 'philosophies' discussed by Josephus, the Essenes
take up by far the most space (*War* 2.8.2–13 §§120–61; *Antiquities*
18.1.5 §§18–22). There is also a lengthy description in Philo
(*Quod omnis* 75–87; *Hypothetica*, as quoted in Eusebius, *Preparation
for the Gospel* 8). Yet perhaps the most interesting account which
makes a close correlation between the area of Qumran and the
Essenes is from the Roman writer Pliny the Elder (*Natural
History* 5.73):

> On the west side of the Dead Sea, but out of range of the noxious
> exhalations of the coast, is the solitary tribe of the Essenes, which is
> remarkable beyond all the other tribes in the whole world, as it has
> no women and has renounced all sexual desire, has no money, and
> has only palm-trees for company . . . Lying below the Essenes was
> formerly the town of Engedi . . . Next comes Masada . . .

The description by Pliny is one of the reasons that the Qumran
community has been identified with the Essenes since shortly

after the discovery of the Dead Sea Scrolls. There are also many points in common between the Essenes as described by Philo and Josephus and the practices described in such Qumran documents as the *Community Rule* and the *Damascus Document*. Not everyone agrees that the Qumranites were Essenes, but this is a widespread view. On the other hand, archaeology indicates that no more than 200 individuals lived at Qumran at its largest, whereas both Philo and Josephus gives the Essene numbers as about 4000. If Qumran was Essene, it was not the totality of the Essene movement. Was it a headquarters or monastery or elite settlement of the Essenes? Was it a breakaway group of Essenes who had left the main community? Was it only a related group? Only some possibilities can be ruled out in the present state of study.

One factor which makes the Essenes and the Qumran group of interest is the fact that both focused on study of the written word and its interpretation. The priests were given pre-eminence in the Qumran community as, for example, in the *Messianic Rule* which lists the duties of the members of the Community (lQS^a):

> [1:13] At the age of thirty years he may approach to participate in lawsuits and judgements, and may take his place among the chiefs of the Thousands of Israel . . . the Judges and the officers of their tribes, in all their families [under the authority] of the sons of [Aar]on the Priests . . . [1:22] The sons of Levi shall hold office, each in his place, under the authority of the sons of Aaron. They shall cause all the congregation to go and come, each man in his rank . . . under the authority of the sons of Zadok the Priests . . .

The *Damascus Covenant* gives the priests the first rank in the community (CD 3:21–4:12). This is made even more explicit in the *Community Rule* where the priests are leaders of the Congregation. They give the blessings, they lead in the rituals, they go first in processions, and have precedence in the assemblies. They are also the guardians of the law and givers of counsel:

> [1QS 5:8–9] He [the new member] shall undertake by a binding oath to return with all his heart and soul to every commandment of the Law of Moses in accordance with all that has been revealed of it

to the sons of Zadok, the Priests, Keepers of the Covenant and Seekers of His will . . .

[1QS 6:3–6] Wherever there are ten men of the Council of the Community there shall not lack a Priest among them. And they shall all sit before him according to their rank and shall be asked their counsel in all things in that order. And when the table has been prepared for eating, and the new wine for drinking, the Priest shall be the first to stretch out his hand to bless the first-fruits of the bread and new wine.

Josephus mentions their study only in passing, but Philo emphasizes how they studied the Law and interpreted it – 'allegorically', as he puts it in *Quod omnis* 80–82:

But the ethical part they study very industriously, taking for trainers the laws of their fathers, which could not possibly have been conceived by the human soul without divine inspiration. In these they are instructed at all other times, but particularly on the seventh days . . . For most of their philosophical study takes the form of allegory, and in this they emulate the tradition of the past.

2.9 Conclusions

A variety of groups and professions within Judaism were concerned with the text of the law. People have to some extent been aware of the place of scribes and have also focused on the different sects such as the Pharisees and Sadducees. What is often overlooked is the important place occupied by the priests in Jewish society, Jewish religion, and scriptural interpretation. Through much of the Second Temple period the priests headed the administrative structures of the community, even holding the office of king during the period of Hasmonaean rule. They were also the ones with the education and the leisure for intellectual pursuits in a way not open to the average son of Israel.

Even in the sectarian Essene community, it is the 'sons of Zadok' who have the primary duty of leadership, counsel, and interpretation of the law. None of these things was limited to priests, but they had the advantage. As for the practice of religion, the centre of pre-70 Judaism was the temple. Again, this is too frequently forgotten in discussions of Judaism of the time. There was more to religion than just the temple, but the temple cult was the bedrock of worship for those in Palestine and the prime symbol of Judaism to those in the Diaspora.

The three main sectarian groups all had a keen interest in the law and its interpretation, though we know much less about each of them with any certainty than is sometimes realized. The Pharisees supplemented the written law with 'traditions of the elders'. Indications in the NT and rabbinic literature suggest that these traditions primarily concerned eating, agricultural laws, festival celebrations, purity, and what anthropologists call the 'exchange of women'. The Pharisees are presented as a group often seeking power in religion and government, but the only time they seem to have succeeded in gaining control is for about a decade under Alexandra Salome (76–67 BCE). Otherwise, whatever their general influence, they did not control the temple (which was under priestly authority) nor did they dominate the civil government (though some individual Pharisees may have had important positions at times). Whether they were a lay movement as is so often asserted remains to be seen; one could argue that it was a priestly movement (it certainly included priests).

The Sadducees and Boethusians are known only from a very little information, and the extant sources are mainly hostile to them (as have been modern scholars, by and large). But one of the strongest inferences from the sources is that they had some connection with the priesthood. Again, the written law was central to their worldview, though they no doubt had their own tradition of interpretation. Some of the more influential men of Jewish society were said to be Sadducees, including apparently at least one Hasmonaean king and one high priest.

We have the fullest description of the Essenes, but there are still many questions, especially with regard to their relationship to the Qumran community. The consensus is still that the Qumran group was Essene, despite some strong criticisms in recent years. The Essenes had a reputation for pious living, an ascetic lifestyle, and the ability to predict the future. Similarly, the

Qumran texts show a group with a great deal of interest in biblical interpretation and prophecy, and the many examples of *pesharim* and other examples of textual exegesis attest the pivotal role of the text in their version of Judaism.

2.10 Guide to Further Reading

The major sects and groups of early Judaism are discussed in Grabbe, *Judaic Religion in the Second Temple Period,* ch. 9 (see also the earlier discussion in *Judaism from Cyrus to Hadrian,* ch. 8). A general discussion of the scribes, sages, and priests in the society of ancient Israel is given in:

> Grabbe, Lester L. *Priests, Prophets, Diviners, Sages: A Socio-historical Study of Religious Specialists in Ancient Israel* (Valley Forge, PA: Trinity Press International, in the press).

For a general discussion of the book of Leviticus and the sacrificial system portrayed in the OT, see:

> Grabbe, Lester L. *Leviticus* (Society for Old Testament Study, Old Testament Guides; Sheffield: JSOT Press, 1993)

On the question of synagogues, probably the best overall treatment is:

> Binder, Donald D. *Into the Temple Courts: The Place of the Synagogues in the Second Temple Period* (SBL Dissertation Series 169; Atlanta: Scholars Press, 1999).

On the priestly governance of Judah, especially by the high priest, see the recent study:

> Goodblatt, David. *The Monarchic Principle: Studies in Jewish Self-Government in Antiquity* (Texte und Studien zum Antiken Judentum 38; Tübingen: Mohr, 1994), though

this needs correction with regard to the 'Sanhedrin'; see the following study:

Grabbe, Lester L. 'Sanhedrin, Sanhedriyyot, or Mere Invention?' *Journal for the Study of Judaism* 39 (2008), 1–19.

VanderKam, James C. 2004 *From Joshua to Caiaphas: High Priests after the Exile* (Minneapolis, MN: Fortress; Assen: Van Gorcum).

On the wise and the wisdom tradition, see Grabbe, *Priests, Prophets, Diviners, Sages,* ch. 6, and the literature cited there. Basic studies include:

Crenshaw, James L. *Old Testament Wisdom: An Introduction* (Louisville: John Knox; London: SCM, 1982).

Whybray, R. N. *The Intellectual Tradition in the Old Testament* (BZAW 135; Berlin/New York: de Gruyter, 1974)

On education in Israel, see the discussion in Grabbe, *Priests, Prophets, Diviners, Sages,* 6.4.3 (pp. 190–96), and the literature cited there. Of special importance is the following study:

Jamieson-Drake, David W. *Scribes and Schools in Monarchic Judah: A Socio-Archeological Approach* (JSOTSup 109; Social World of Biblical Antiquity 9; Sheffield: Almond Press, 1991).

An important study on the various sects is:

Saldarini, Anthony J. *Pharisees, Scribes and Sadducees in Palestinian Society: A Sociological Approach* (Wilmington, DE: Glazier, 1988).

The classic work on the Pharisees remains:

Neusner, Jacob. *From Politics to Piety: The Emergence of Pharisaic Judaism* (Englewood Cliffs, NJ: Prentice-Hall, 1973).

For a history of the Qaraites, see:

Nemoy, Leon, et al. 'Karaites', *Encyclopaedia Judaica* (New York: Macmillan, 1971) vol. 10, pp. 761–85.

On the scribes, in addition to Grabbe, *Judaism from Cyrus to Hadrian* (pp. 488-91), see especially:

Schams, Christine. *Jewish Scribes in the Second-Temple Period* (Journal for the Study of the Old Testament Supplement 291; Sheffield Academic Press, 1998).

CHAPTER 3

⎯⎯⎯⎯⎯

REVOLUTIONARY JUDAISM:
THE POLITICAL AND
'MESSIANIC' CURRENT

3.1 Introduction

A traditional Jewish belief was that the descendants of Israel had once constituted a great nation which had conquered and controlled a large part of the Eastern Mediterranean world. The Jews remembered that under David and Solomon, they had subdued the surrounding nations and had established dominance from the River of Egypt to the Euphrates. It is hardly surprising that this was widely believed by the Jewish people in antiquity – even many modern scholars have embraced this view, though some trenchant recent studies label it a mere legend.

Such a powerful element in the national mythology was likely to have an effect at some point. Yet for centuries after the conquest of Jerusalem by Nebuchadnezzar's army in 587/586 BCE, the Jewish nation seems to have submitted to foreign domination. They had learned well the lesson of the destruction of the First Temple and the Jewish monarchy. They became just another small nation under the thumb of large Mesopotamian powers. In reality Judah had been under Assyrian rule for much of the last century even of the monarchy. The Assyrians fell before the Neo-Babylonians, but Babylonian rule lasted only a half century or so, to be replaced by the Persians. The Persians held sway for over two centuries before the Greeks, under Alexander, defeated Darius III and established their own empire. Although the Greeks were European, much of Greek rule was subsumed under the Seleucid and Ptolemaic empires which were true heirs of the Near Eastern empires before them.

Judah was only a small country in the shadow of the great powers. The Jews were hardly in a position to challenge the ruling empires. Rebellion did occasionally take place among some of the subordinate nations – periodic revolt seems to have been the norm in Egypt, for example – but it was usually ineffective. It has been alleged there was a Jewish rebellion under the Persians, known as the Tennes rebellion, but this reconstruction has been challenged. It is very uncertain, at best. Otherwise, between the fall of Jerusalem and the Maccabaean revolt, Judah followed what was no doubt the wisest course: submission to the inevitable. This all changed in the quarter of a century after the Seleucids took over.

3.2 The Maccabaean Revolt

As has already been discussed (in section 1.1.5), the Maccabaean revolt was a very unusual event. The causes of the revolt were no doubt multiple, but the key event was Antiochus IV's suppression of Jewish worship. The Books of 1 and 2 Maccabees give a partisan, pro-Maccabaean perspective. Enough hints about political manoeuvring between various resistance groups are present to make us wonder, but the detailed intricacies are probably lost forever. All that is left is the account which elevates the Maccabaean brothers, especially Judas; whether it was quite that simple is another question. The Maccabaean resistance is presented as holy war in 1 Maccabees, and their victories as due to a combination of personal astuteness and bravery and of divine intervention. The actual reasons are likely to be more prosaic.

In the long history of military engagements, many unusual things have happened, and one or two Maccabaean victories may be enumerated among these. Most of their wins are fully explicable in the light of normal military factors, however: equal or superior numbers of troops, the tactic of surprise, the knowledge of local terrain, the development of a trained regular army. Guerrilla tactics were used of necessity in the early part of the resistance, but one of Judas' achievements was to develop a trained and equipped standing army. The stunning success of a small band of Maccabaean irregulars against overwhelming Seleucid odds excites our romantic tendencies, but it is just that – romantic fiction.

Once the temple had been recaptured and Jewish worship again officially recognized by the Seleucid government, many of those who had thrown their lot behind the revolt now made peace with their opponents. Their religious goals had been accomplished, and they had no nationalistic ones. Not so the Maccabees who came to want nothing less than independence for a Jewish state. But many supporters withdrew their support, causing a major setback. Judas himself was killed on the battle-field, and the next decade saw the Maccabees mainly on the run from the Seleucid troops. When they finally succeeded, it was through political measures more than military might. The rise of rival claimants to the Seleucid throne gave Jonathan Maccabee the chance he needed to court each side, gain con-cessions from both, and then eventually side with the highest bidder. After some considerable success at playing this danger-ous game, Jonathan miscalculated and paid the price with his life. His work was carried on by his brother Simon who eventu-ally gained more or less independence from Seleucid rule. The Seleucids never completely gave up their claims, but they had other troubles, and the Hasmonaean Jewish state was born.

The result was that, whatever qualifications one should make, the success of the Maccabees in gaining freedom from Seleucid rule was nevertheless unique, and an independent Jewish state flourished for almost a century. The Jewish people were not going to forget that for a long time to come.

3.3 The Roman Overlords

The Hasmonaean kingdom was brought to an end most imme-diately by its own actions. Two brothers, Aristobulus II and Hyrcanus II, were rivals for the throne, and each appealed to the Roman legate Pompey who was in Syria at the time. Pompey ultimately sided with Hyrcanus. Aristobulus threatened resist-ance but then surrendered; his followers held out in Jerusalem, however, and the Romans took it in 63 BCE. Although Hyrcanus was declared the nominal leader of the Jews, Judah was now under Roman rule. Its brief period as a sovereign nation had come to an end.

The trauma of this loss of independence and power was considerable. Some Jews found a bit of grim satisfaction in the defeat and death of Pompey, the uncircumcised unbeliever who not only conquered Jerusalem but even went into the Holy of Holies of the temple after slaughtering priests at the altar (see section 1.1.6). Yet the realities were that Judah had no choice but to submit to Rome. This does not mean that all Jews were reconciled to the idea, however; the infamous conquest of Jerusalem only began a series of abortive revolts against Rome. This was the turbulent period of the Late Roman Republic with powerful rival factions fighting each other to the death, using the entire Roman world as their stage. So a revolt in Judah might well succeed under the right circumstances, at least temporarily.

Aristobulus was himself taken to Rome as a hostage, but his two sons Alexander and Antigonus were allowed to remain with their mother who appealed to Pompey directly. First, Alexander led an attack on Hyrcanus II and is alleged to have raised 10,000 heavy infantry and 1500 cavalry. He was defeated only with Roman help. The very next year Aristobulus himself escaped, along with Antigonus, and led a new revolt, raising an army of similar size to that of Alexander. Again, the Romans defeated him and returned him to Rome. Alexander and Antigonus were released by the Senate, and Alexander immediately revolted again, without success.

In the sources from the time, it is not always easy to distinguish between ordinary brigands and 'revolutionaries'. The reason is that most writers were figures of the establishment and to them there was little distinction. Also, the lifestyle of the two might not necessarily be that different. To the people themselves and to modern sociologists, however, there was and is an importance difference. Thus, the term 'bandit' (*lēstēs*) in a literary work might refer to one who simply earned his living by robbing and raiding, or it might refer to one opposing the ruling power for ideological reasons. Josephus was no different from other Graeco-Roman writers. He detested the 'revolutionaries' who brought about the destruction of Jerusalem and the country – at least, with hindsight he did, though he was one himself for a certain period of time. In any case, it is not always clear whether his bandits are of the common-or-garden variety or of the revolutionary kind.

One of those labelled a bandit by Josephus was Ezekias (Hezekiah) who was raiding in the area along the Syrian border in the middle of the first century BCE. As governor of Galilee Herod captured and executed him and many of his followers (*War* 1.10.5 §204). Later on, after he had been declared king, Herod conducted a winter campaign against the numerous brigands who lived in caves northwest of the Sea of Galilee. They met him with what seems to have been a regular army rather than with the expected guerrilla tactics, suggesting a good deal of organization. Despite their rather formidable initial attack he routed them (*War* 1.16.2–3 §§304–7). Those who fled to the safety of their cave retreats were much harder to deal with, but he also succeeded in exterminating them (*War* 1.16.4 §§309–13).

Were these ordinary bandits or revolutionaries? Josephus gives no hint that they were the latter, but we cannot be sure. In this case, they refused to surrender but perished to the last man, woman, and child. This suggests more than ordinary brigandage. Perhaps the group in Galilee was in some way associated with the insurrection of Antigonus which was under way at the time (see above). For as soon as Herod had got rid of the cave bandits, another revolt broke out in Galilee which he had to deal with (*War* 1.16.5 §§314–16). Some months later when Herod had a setback in his fight, the supporters of Antigonus in Galilee killed the local leadership who supported Herod (*War* 1.17.2 §§325–26). If nothing else, this illustrates the problem with trying to interpret the historical sources.

As a peripheral point, it has sometimes been suggested that Galileans were particularly prone to revolutionary movements. Although certain revolutionaries are associated with Galilee, there is no clear evidence that it was more subject to them than other parts of greater Judaea.

3.4 Revolts during the 'War of Varus'

As soon as Herod the Great died in 4 BCE, a wave of unrest surged through Palestine. Herod's son Archelaus quickly put down the demonstrations, with the aid of Roman troops as well as Herod's army. Then the various sons travelled to Rome to put their cases before Augustus – each hoping to succeed his father. While they were away, unrest continued to simmer for a time and then broke into a series of revolts. The Roman commander Sabinus called for help from the legions commanded by Varus, the imperial legate in Syria. The situation was clearly serious, and a large force was called in to quell what might turn into a general rebellion. Some of these were people who apparently had political motives; for example, some of Herod's own veterans revolted. But others seem to have been driven by ideological motives, at least in part. Josephus tells us of several leaders at this time (*War* 2.4.1–3 §§56–65):

> At Sepphoris in Galilee Judas, son of Ezechias, the brigand-chief who in former days infested the country and was subdued by King Herod, raised a considerable body of followers, broke open the royal arsenals, and, having armed his companions, attacked the other aspirants to power. In Peraea Simon, one of the royal slaves, proud of his tall and handsome figure, assumed the diadem. Perambulating the country with the brigands whom he had collected, he burnt down the royal palace at Jericho and many other stately mansions, such incendiarism providing him with an easy opportunity for plunder . . . Now, too, a mere shepherd had the temerity to aspire to the throne. He was called Athrongaeus, and his sole recommendations, to raise such hopes, were vigour of body, a soul contemptuous of death, and four brothers resembling himself. To each of these he entrusted an armed band and employed them as generals and satraps for his raids, while he himself, like a king, handled matters of graver moment. It was now that he donned the diadem, but his raiding expeditions throughout the country with his brothers continued long afterwards. Their principal object was to kill Romans and royalists, but no Jew, from whom they had anything to gain, escaped, if he fell into their hands.

3.5 The 'Fourth Philosophy' and the Sicarii

When Judaea became a Roman province in 6 CE, a census was taken (mistakenly dated in Luke 2:1–3 to the time of Herod's reign). Many Jews protested against this, but the bulk of the people gradually acquiesced after intervention by the high priest. Josephus writes (*Antiquities* 18.1.1 §§4–10):

> But a certain Judas, a Gaulanite from a city named Gamala, who had enlisted the aid of Saddok, a Pharisee, threw himself into the cause of rebellion. They said that the assessment carried with it a status amounting to downright slavery, no less, and appealed to the nation to make a bid for independence. They urged that in case of success the Jews would have laid the foundation of prosperity, while if they failed to obtain any such boon, they would win honour and renown for their lofty aim; and that Heaven would be their zealous helper to no lesser end than the furthering of their enterprise until it succeeded – all the more if with high devotion in their hearts they stood firm and did not shrink from the bloodshed that might be necessary. Since the populace, when they heard their appeals, responded gladly, the plot to strike boldly made serious progress; and so these men sowed the seed of every kind of misery, which so afflicted the nation that words are inadequate . . . In this case certainly, Judas and Saddok started among us an intrusive fourth school of philosophy; and when they had won an abundance of devotees, they filled the body politic immediately with tumult, also planting the seeds of those troubles which subsequently overtook it, all because of the novelty of this hitherto unknown philosophy that I shall now describe.

He also suggests that the 'Fourth Philosophy' gave rise to the Sicarii in the 40s. The Sicarii took their name from a type of dagger, called the *sica* in Latin. One might with good reason translate their name as 'Assassins'. They would conceal the dagger inside their clothing, get close to an official in the throng, strike quickly, and slip back into the crowd before being apprehended. This is what Josephus says about their connections with the Fourth Philosophy (*Antiquities* 18.1.6 §§23–25):

> As for the fourth of the philosophies, Judas the Galilaean set himself up as leader of it. This school agrees in all other respects with the opinions of the Pharisees, except that they have a passion for

liberty that is almost unconquerable, since they are convinced that God alone is their leader and master . . . The folly that ensued began to afflict the nation after Gessius Florus, who was governor, had by his overbearing and lawless actions provoked a desperate rebellion against the Romans.

Whether or not he should be believed about the origins of the Sicarii is a matter of debate since Josephus was unsympathetic to the various revolutionary groups and might want to see them as all connected. If he is right, however, there was a line stretching from Ezekias to Judas the Galilean and on to the Sicarii, showing a continuous family 'Mafia' extending for 75 years or more.

This is further indicated in the early part of the revolt by the leader of the Sicarii who was named Menahem (*War* 2.17.8–9 §§433–48):

At this period a certain Menahem, son of Judas surnamed the Galilaean – that redoubtable doctor who in old days, under Quirinius, had upbraided the Jews for recognizing the Romans as masters when they already had God – took his intimate friends off with him to Masada, where he broke into king Herod's armoury and provided arms both for his fellow-townsmen and for other brigands; then, with these men for his bodyguard, he returned like a veritable king to Jerusalem, became the leader of the revolution, and directed the siege of the palace . . . On the following day the high-priest Ananias was caught near the canal in the palace grounds, where he was hiding, and, with his brother Ezechias, was killed by the brigands . . . But the reduction of the strongholds and the murder of the high-priest Ananias inflated and brutalized Menahem to such an extent that he believed himself without a rival in the conduct of affairs and became an insufferable tyrant. The partisans of Eleazar now rose against him . . . So they laid their plans to attack him in the Temple, whither he had gone up in state to pay his devotions, arrayed in royal robes and attended by his suite of armed fanatics.

Menahem himself was thus killed very early during the war. The Sicarii as a whole then abandoned Jerusalem and holed up at Masada and were not involved further in the war. It was after the fall of Jerusalem that the Romans decided that this last rebel faction had to be removed. The details of the final siege of Masada can be gleaned to some extent from archaeology, and there are many who argue that Josephus' account – despite its romantic appeal – is highly legendary.

3.6 *The Zealots and the 66–70 War*

The two decades after the death of Agrippa I in 44 saw a gradual but inexorable slide into war. It had been a century since the Hasmonaean kingdom had come to an end, but the Jewish Hasmonaean state was no doubt still firm in folk memory. Agrippa's short-lived reign had evidently been popular, but Claudius refused to allow his son Agrippa II to succeed him. Claudius presumably had his reasons; he said it was because of Agrippa's youth, but this may have been only a pretext. This meant the return of unpopular direct Roman rule. The series of Roman governors which followed was not calculated to soothe the apprehensions of the Jewish people. By all reports – Roman as well as Jewish – they were by and large a corrupt, insensitive, and incompetent lot. There may have been exceptions such as Julius Tiberius Alexander, a member of a leading Jewish family in Alexander (though Josephus claims that he left his ancestral religion), but the general experience was evidently quite negative.

During this time the Sicarii were quite active. In addition to killing Jewish officials, they took to kidnapping important officials (e.g. members of the high priest's family) and holding them for ransom. Despite suffering from these crimes, some of the high priests were also alleged to have hired the Sicarii to do some of their dirty work. Even certain of the Roman governors reportedly availed themselves of the Sicarii talents! (The Sicarii generally avoided clashes with the Romans, preferring to assassinate Jews who were seen as collaborators rather than make attempts on Roman officials.)

The causes of the revolt were probably multiple. Apart from the unsatisfactory governors, the Jewish leadership seems to have failed its own people. National mythology was also likely to have played an important role; that is, Jewish memory of their free and autonomous past, suitably embroidered and idealized, was a constant reminder of how much below that model state was their present situation. They had been free – they could be free again! Had not Judas Maccabeus and his brave band defeated great odds by divine help? Religious beliefs and expectations were clearly a prime mover behind the revolt when it came. As the event which began the war some have pointed to the decision by Eleazar b. Ananias, who held the office of captain (*stratēgos*) of the temple, to cancel the daily sacrifices on behalf of the Roman emperor (*War* 2.17.2–3 §§409–16). This decision was important for its high symbolic value, though it is difficult to take one single event as *the* cause of the war – there was a whole chain of events.

It was during this revolt that the group called the Zealots first becomes apparent. There is a debate on the use of the term 'zealot' (from Greek *zēlotēs*). The term may be used generically for anyone who displayed zeal in devotion to God like that of Phinehas (Numbers 25), and for this reason some have used it indiscriminately to refer to any revolutionary group. However, Josephus clearly uses the term primarily in reference to a particular group who had themselves taken this name. This group was particularly active in Jerusalem before and during the siege. Josephus says about them (*War* 4.3.3–9 §§135–61):

> [135] In the end, satiated with their pillage of the country, the brigand chiefs of all these scattered bands joined forces and, now merged into one pack of villainy, stole into poor Jerusalem . . . [138] Fresh brigands from the country entering the city and joining the yet more formidable gang within, abstained henceforth from no enormities . . . [158] This latest outrage was more than the people could stand, and as if for the overthrow of a despotism one and all were now roused . . . [160] Their efforts were supported by the most eminent of the high priests, Jesus, son of Gamalas, and Ananus, son of Ananus, who at their meetings vehemently upbraided the people for their apathy and incited them against the Zealots; for so these miscreants called themselves, as though they were zealous in the cause of virtue and not for vice in its basest and most extravagant form.

It is therefore unhelpful to lump all these various groups together as Zealots (with a capital letter), even if they tended to have certain characteristics in common.

The earlier history of the Zealots is unknown. Some have argued that they first formed about 68 CE from a coalition of resistance groups who withdrew to Jerusalem, as noted in the quotation above. On the other hand, there may be a reference to their existence already as early as the beginning of the war in late 66 or early 67 (*War* 2.2.1 §651):

> Ananus, nevertheless, cherished the thought of gradually abandoning these warlike preparations and bending the malcontents and the infatuated so-called zealots to a more salutary policy; but he succumbed to their violence, and the sequel of our narrative will show the fate which befell him.

The question is whether 'zealot' here is a proper name or only an epithet. The context suggests a name; if so, there is nothing to rule out a longer history. What is clear is that they should not be confused with the Sicarii, whose history is better known (see section 3.5); even if the Zealots may have had some organic connection with the Fourth Philosophy/Sicarii at some point, they are kept separate by Josephus. The Zealots fought bravely and fanatically in the final siege of Jerusalem, and most of them perished in the battle. The Sicarii had left Jerusalem long before. It was they, not the Zealots, who held out at Masada, despite Yadin's confusing reference to that last holdout against Rome as Zealot.

One of the reasons that the term Zealots should not be used confusedly of all groups is that a number of these parties fought one another before the Romans finally tightened the siege. There were several factional leaders rivalling one another in the final months of the war. The result was that even while Titus was preparing the final siege of Jerusalem, three separate groups controlled different portions of the city and fought each other ferociously. Josephus summarizes the situation at the beginning of his Book 5 (*War* 5.1.1–3 §§1–20):

> Of the Zealots' attack upon the populace – the first step towards the city's ruin – a precise account has already been given, showing its origin and all the mischief in which it culminated [John of Gischala was now leader of the Zealots] . . . For Eleazar, son of Simon, the man who had originally caused the Zealots to break with

the citizens and withdraw into the sacred precincts, now . . . seceded from the party, taking with him Judes son of Chelcias, and Simon son of Esron, persons of weight, along with a man of some distinction, Ezechias son of Chobari. Each of these having a considerable following of Zealots, the seceders took possession of the inner court of the temple and planted their weapons above the holy gates on the sacred facade . . . but they were daunted by the paucity of their numbers and as a rule sat still and held their ground. On the other hand, John's numerical superiority was counterbalanced by the inferiority of his position . . . Then there was Simon, son of Gioras, whom the people in their straits had summoned in hope of relief, only to impose upon themselves a further tyrant. He occupied the Upper and a large part of the Lower City, and now attacked John's party more vigorously, seeing that they were also assailed from above; but he was attacking them beneath, as were they their foes higher up.

One of the real puzzles about the revolt is that instead of putting their energies into fighting the Romans, they wasted several years fighting each other and exploiting the refugees who had come to Jerusalem. The Romans had first attacked and taken Galilee. At this point, the fighters from there and the outlying regions all moved to Jerusalem. Yet already the Zealots seem to have forgotten about the Romans and to concentrate on gaining power in the city. I find this very puzzling because it goes against reality as well as their whole reason for revolting in the first place. Almost our only source is Josephus who strongly opposed these groups, at least by the time he came to write about them some years later. Is there something he does not tell us? Was there some sort of religious view that God would not let Jerusalem fall because his temple and dwelling was there (the so-called belief in the 'inviolability of Zion' known to have been maintained by some during the First Temple period – cf. Isaiah 8:5–10; 30:27–33; 33:5–6,14–24)? Was there a strong expectation that the eschaton was at hand? At least some Jews seem to have believed this, even at the time the city was falling to the Romans (*War* 6.5.2 §§283–86):

They [the Romans] then proceeded to the one remaining portico of the outer court, on which the poor women and children of the populace and a mixed multitude had taken refuge, numbering six thousand . . . They owed their destruction to a false prophet, who had on that day proclaimed to the people in the city that God commanded them to go up to the temple court, to receive there the tokens of their deliverance. Numerous prophets, indeed, were at this period suborned by the tyrants to delude the people, by bidding them await help from God, in order that desertions might be checked and that those who were above fear and precaution might be encouraged by hope.

Further indications that this refusal to face military reality was based on an apocalyptic belief are found in another passage of Josephus about some 'ambiguous oracles'. See further at section 4.6.2.

3.7 The Bar Kokhba Revolt

When Josephus wrote his first book, the *War of the Jews,* one of his aims was to show the Jews that the might of Rome was undefeatable and any rebellion was foolish. One might have thought that this point was unnecessary to make since the Jews had surely learned their lesson – with their city and temple in ruins. But Josephus' instinct was correct. In less than 50 years the Jews of Egypt and Mesopotamia tried their own chance for independence, just as unsuccessfully as their brethren in Palestine. It has even been suggested that the Palestinian Jews joined in, but there is little evidence for this. The 115–17 revolts are known from only a few brief sources, but they seem to have involved many members of the Jewish communities in each of these areas.

The Jews of Palestine took their turn once again in 132. As with previous revolts, the causes were complex, but one contributing factor was probably the lack of total defeat in 66–70. Many Jews had been killed, but much of the death and destruction was centred on Jerusalem. The rest of the country seems to have got off relatively lightly, and the economy recovered fairly rapidly. It was the total defeat and the massive destruction of the 132–35 war which put paid to any hopes of a revived Jewish state for another 1800 years.

Sadly, we lack a detailed account of the Bar Kokhba war. It must be pieced together from a few brief literary descriptions, some further passing references in Graeco-Roman literature, several legendary accounts in rabbinic literature, and the invaluable finds of coins and other archaeological evidence and the letters and documents among the Dead Sea Scrolls. These leave a number of loose ends.

The war itself was apparently under way at least as early as the spring of 132, and it seems to have continued into the fourth year, to the autumn of 135. For once, the figure of three and a half years, so well known from biblical literature (Daniel 7:25; Revelation 11:2–3; 13:5), may actually have been correct. The centre of Bar Kokhba's activities was the Judaean desert west of the Dead Sea. The oasis of Engedi seems to have been an important base, with vegetation, water, and a potential inlet for supplies by boat. It has been proposed that Jerusalem was even taken and held temporarily, but this now seems unlikely. However, there is some evidence that Jewish fighters used underground tunnels and bunkers to hide from the enemy and to carry out surprise attacks.

One of the puzzles is the question of whether Bar Kokhba claimed to be the Messiah. The revolt is named for the leader whom we now know to be called Simon ben Kosiba. He had the epithet Bar Kokhba (Aramaic 'son of the star') applied to him according to tradition, and it is by this name that he is still remembered. The 'star' of the title is associated with the star of Numbers 24, suggesting a messianic claim on his part. Some symbols on the Bar Kokhba coins have also been interpreted in this way. On the other hand, the letters and other documents from the Judaean desert are quite prosaic. Bar Kokhba takes care of ordinary business affairs; he writes about military matters; he seems to be a normal leader. No messianic titles are used; no indications of larger-than-life claims appear in his letters and papers. Here is one of his letters (Murabba'at 44):

> [From Sh]imon (ben Kosiba) to Yeshua son of Galgula: Greetings: You are to send five ko[r]-measures of [wheat by me]n of my house who are known to you. Prepare for them an empty place. They will be with you this sabbath, if they desire to come. Keep up your

courage and strengthen that place. Best wishes. I have designated
the person who is to give yo[u] his [whe]at. They may take it after
the sabbath.

This leads to the question of messianic expectations in general
as a basis for at least some revolts.

3.8 Messianic Expectations

I use the term 'messianic' with some trepidation. The modern
belief in the importance of 'messianic expectations' in the first
century is extremely strong and widespread, despite a number
of warning voices raised by those specialists who best know the
literature. The reason seems to be a particular understanding of
the NT in general and Jesus in particular. The Greek title *christos*
('anointed') became applied to Jesus within the decades after
his death. Some Gospel passages also picture him as being asked
whether he was 'the Christ' – evidently a reference to a Jewish
belief in the coming of a Messiah. The problem for the scholar
of early Judaism is, first, that the Gospels have their own agenda,
centring on Jesus and the development of Christology and,
then, the apparent assumption that there was a strong and
single view of the Messiah among the Jews at this time.

The term Messiah comes from Hebrew *māšîăḥ*, a passive form
meaning 'anointed'. In the OT it was used primarily of the king
or the high priest, though Cyrus the Persian king is also called
God's anointed (Isaiah 45:1). The later development of the concept of Messiah is influenced by this origin; in fact, it has been
argued that two themes running through texts which feature a
Messiah are those of the king-priest and the warrior-judge. Both
of these arise from the priestly and kingly traditions. Despite
the apparent importance of these themes, we need to recognize
the variety of views about the Messiah which do not form a
coherent whole – which cannot be reduced to a single 'Jewish
messianic expectation' in the late Second Temple period. One
of the methodological failings in so many treatments is to speak
of 'messianism' or 'messianic expectations' in texts which do
not use the word Messiah in any way. Some of these passages
may be relevant, but this is very much a subjective judgement.

Thus, the texts of relevance for this chapter are those that have only one particular view of the Messiah and are only a portion of those which speak of such a figure. These are the texts which feature a Messiah as one who rules on earth, whether in the king-priest mode or the warrior-judge mode. (Those which seem to picture a heavenly figure are dealt with in the next chapter, in section 4.7.) The first of these is found in the *Psalms of Solomon* 17:

> [17:23] Behold, O Lord, and raise up for them their king, the son of David, For the time which thou didst foresee, O God, that he may reign over Israel thy servant.
>
> And gird him with strength, that he may shatter unrighteous rulers; And purify Jerusalem of the nations which trample her down in destruction. In wisdom, in righteousness, may he expel sinners from the inheritance:
>
> May he smash the sinner's arrogance like a potter's vessel. With a rod of iron may he break in pieces all their substance: May he destroy the lawless nations by the word of his mouth, So that, at his rebuke, nations flee before him; And may he reprove sinners by the word of their own hearts. And he shall gather together a holy people, whom he shall lead in righteousness, And he shall judge the tribes of the people which has been sanctified by the Lord his God . . .
>
> [17:32] And he shall have the peoples of the Gentiles to serve him under his yoke; And he shall glorify the Lord at the centre of all the earth, And he shall purify Jerusalem . . .
>
> [17:35] And he shall be a righteous king, taught by God, over them, And there shall be no unrighteousness in his days in their midst, For all shall be holy, and their king the anointed Lord.

Some passages in the Gospels seem to imply that some Jews expected a conquering Messiah who would free Israel from her oppressors. For example, Jesus is asked this by the disciples in Acts 1:6–7:

> So when they had come together, they asked him, 'Lord, is this the time when you will restore the kingdom to Israel?' He replied, 'It is not for you to know the times or periods that the Father has set by his own authority.'

The views of the Qumran community are not completely clear. The *War Scroll* (1QM) describes a series of eschatological battles between the Sons of Light and the Sons of Darkness. Although there is a standoff for the first part of the war, the Sons of Light eventually triumph. The weapons may be divine, but the battle is real. Yet this writing says nothing about a messianic figure.

On the other hand, a variety of eschatalogical figures occurs in the Qumran texts. The *Damascus Document* speaks of 'the Messiah of Aaron and Israel' (CD 12:23–13:1). Is this meant to be one Messiah or two? CD 19:10–11 seems to have one figure in mind when it refers to 'the Messiah from Aaron and Israel'. On the other hand, the *Community Rule* speaks of 'the prophet and the Messiahs of Aaron and Israel' (1QS 9:11). In none of these passages is the function of the Messiah described. The passages which refer specifically to a Messiah or Messiahs are few and somewhat unspecific. Another important passage is found in the document sometimes referred to as the *Alessianic Rule* (lQS^a). Here a Messiah of Aaron (priestly Messiah) and a Messiah of Israel seem to be envisaged:

> [2:11] When God will have engendered [the Priest-] Messiah, he shall come [at] the head of the whole congregation of Israel with all [his brethren, the sons] of Aaron the Priests . . . And then [the Mess]iah of Israel shall [come], and the chiefs of the [clans of Israel] shall sit before him . . . let no man extend his hand over the first-fruits of bread and wine before the Priest; for [it is he] who shall bless the first-fruits of bread and wine, and shall be the first [to extend] his hand over the bread. Thereafter, the Messiah of Israel shall extend his hand over the bread, [and] all the congregation of the Community [shall utter a] blessing, [each man in the order] of his dignity.

The Messianic expectations at Qumran seem not to have been a major part of the community's eschatological view. At least, they do not refer to them often, though they are there in the background. It has also been argued – not unreasonably – that their views developed and changed over time, perhaps from the expectation of only one Messianic figure to a situation with several.

The main apocalypses from the end of the first century both have messianic figures, though with some slight differences. In 4 Ezra we are given this picture:

> [7:28] For my son the Messiah shall be revealed with those who are with him, and those who remain shall rejoice four hundred years. After those years my son the Messiah shall die, and all who draw human breath. Then the world shall be turned back to primeval silence for seven days, as it was at the first beginnings, so that no one shall be left. After seven days the world that is not yet awake shall be roused, and that which is corruptible shall perish. The earth shall give up those who are asleep in it, and the dust those who rest there in silence; and the chambers shall give up the souls that have been committed to them.

The messianic age is followed by the final judgement. A passage in 2 Baruch is similar but does not envisage the death of the Messiah, only his gradual revelation and a smooth transition from the Messianic Kingdom into the final Kingdom of God:

> [29:3] And it shall be that when all is accomplished that was to come to pass in the twelve periods before the end, the Messiah shall then begin to be revealed . . . The earth also shall yield its fruit ten thousand-fold; and on each vine there shall be a thousand branches, and each branch shall produce a thousand clusters, and each cluster produce a thousand grapes, and each grape produce a cor of wine . . . [30:1] And it shall come to pass after this, when the time of the presence of the Messiah on earth has run its course, that he will return in glory to the heavens: then all who have died and have set their hopes on him will rise again.

3.9 Conclusions

A strong core of resistance thought is found through part of the history of Second Temple Judaism. Under Persian and Ptolemaic rule we find little evidence that the Jews attempted any sort of revolt against their overlords. There are probably two reasons for this: first, it was most likely recognized that any revolt had little chance of success since Judah was only a small province with few resources; secondly, they (like all other peoples in these empires) had the opportunity to practise their religion freely and without hinderance. Expectations of some sort of future Davidic ruler were still probably maintained, at least in some circles, since this was a part of the prophetic literature. But if so, it does not seem to have generated any active attempt to break free from foreign rule.

A change of attitude came when the Jews were no longer allowed to exercise their religion: they would tolerate a lot of things but not religious suppression. When Antiochus attempted to impose another cult in place of the traditional one, the hitherto peaceful Jewish people revolted. This began a tradition of resistance to foreign rule which then continued as a powerful current through the next three centuries until the decisive defeat under Bar Kokhba put a definite end to such ideas. This was an undercurrent much of the time, but at opportune moments it broke through to the surface, usually when the grip of their foreign masters temporarily slipped or seemed weak.

Some of the revolts and movements may have been mainly political, with independence the primary goal. But some – and possibly most – were what sociologists call millenarian movements. That is, they had an ideological base. Thus, some opposed foreign rule because they believed that only God could be their ruler. Others thought that God had raised or was about to raise up a messianic figure to lead them into a new world of peace and prosperity for Israel. Our sources do not always make clear the motivations because the literary writers were not infrequently hostile to these movements. What is clear is that from the Maccabees to Bar Kokhba we find a steady tradition of passive opposition and occasionally active resistance to outside rule.

3.10 Guide to Further Reading

For more detailed information on the Maccabaean revolt, see Grabbe, *Judaism from Cyrus to Hadrian*, ch. 5. On the Roman takeover and the revolts against the Romans and Herod, see ch. 6. The 66–70 war against Rome, as well as the events leading up to it, are found in ch. 7, and the Bar Kokhba revolt is in ch. 9. See ch. 8 for sections on 'bandits' (8.2.12; 8.3.5), Zealots (8.2.7),

Fourth Philosophy and Sicarii (8.2.8). For a study of the military engagements during the Maccabaean revolt, see:

Bar-Kochva, B. *Judas Maccabaeus: The Jewish Struggle Against the Seleucids* (Cambridge: Cambridge University Press, 1989).

The best detailed study of the 66–70 war against Rome is:

Price, Jonathan J. *Jerusalem under Siege: The Collapse of the Jewish State 66-70 C.E.* (Brill's Series in Jewish Studies 3; Leiden: Brill, 1992).

The main study of the Zealots is the following, though it uses a broader definition of the term than I feel is acceptable:

Hengel, Martin. *The Zealots: Investigations into the Jewish Freedom Movement in the Period from Herod I until 70 AD* (Edinburgh: T & T Clark, 1989).

The classic study of 'banditry' in the Roman empire is:

Macmullen, Ramsay. *Enemies of the Roman Order: Treason, Unrest, and Alienation in the Empire* (Cambridge, MA: Harvard, 1967; paperback reprint London: Routledge, 1993).

A discussion of the place of Galilee in revolutionary movements is given in:

Freyne, Sean. *Galilee from Alexander the Great to Hadrian: A Study of Second Temple Judaism* (Notre Dame: University of Notre Dame, 1980), pp. 208–47.

On the failure of Jewish leadership in the decades before 70, see:

Goodman, Martin. *The Ruling Class of Judaea: The Origins of the Jewish Revolt against Rome A.D. 66-70* (Cambridge: Cambridge University Press, 1987).

On the letters of Bar-Kokhba (in Hebrew, Aramaic, and Greek, some of which have not yet been published), see the following:

> Pardee, Dennis, et al., *Handbook of Ancient Hebrew Letters* (Society of Biblical Literature Sources for Biblical Study 15; Atlanta: Scholars, 1982).

> Fitzmyer, J. A., and D. J. Harrington, *A Manual of Palestinian Aramaic Texts* (BibOr 34; Rome: Biblical Institute, 1978).

> Lewis, Naphthali (ed.), *The Documents from the Bar Kokhba Period in the Cave of Letters: Greek Papyri*, with Y. Yadin and J. C. Greenfield (ed.) *Aramaic and Nabatean Signatures and Subscriptions* (Jerusalem: Israel Exploration Society, 1989).

The most recent comprehensive study of the Messiah is still the following:

> Oegema, Gerbern S. *The Anointed and his People: Messianic Expectations from the Maccabees to Bar Kochba* (JSPSup 27; Sheffield Academic Press, 1998).

Other important studies are:

> Neusner, J.; W. S. Green; and E. S. Frerichs (eds) *Judaisms and Their Messiahs at the Turn of the Christian Era* (Cambridge: Cambridge University Press, 1987).

> Charlesworth, J. H. (ed.) *The Messiah: Developments in Earliest Judaism and Christianity* (with J. Brownson, M. T. Davis, S. J. Kraftchick, A. F. Segal; The First Princeton Symposium on Judaism and Christian Origins; Minneapolis, MN: Fortress, 1992).

On millenarian movements, with an extensive bibliography of sociological and anthropological studies, see:

> Grabbe, Lester L. 'The Social Setting of Early Jewish Apocalypticism', *Journal for the Study of the Pseudepigrapha* 4 (1989), 27–47.

CHAPTER 4

ESCHATOLOGICAL JUDAISM: THE APOCALYPTIC CURRENT

4.1 Introduction

The term 'eschatology' refers to the concept of the 'last things': the end of life, the end of the world, final judgement, life after death. Death has always been a part of life, and there is much said about it in the OT. Yet the idea that there was life after death seems to have developed only very late in the OT literature. It is generally agreed that for much of the OT writings, death brought the end of the individual as a person. Something survived in Sheol, but the shadowy existence there was not life as such and the shade (*nefeš*) was not the person.

Alongside the 'official' teaching of the literature, though, there may have been other more popular beliefs. The exact form of these beliefs is not entirely clear; indeed, one should probably think of a variety of beliefs rather than a unified doctrine. The indications are that the dead were regarded as having powers and knowledge of the future in some circles. The question is currently being debated; in any case, the view that death could be survived becomes a clear view only in the Persian or Greek periods. It has been suggested that this was primarily due to Zoroastrian or Greek influence, though others have argued that it was a natural development from Israelite roots. Demonstrating the matter one way or the other is difficult, and there is no reason to rule out any of these possibilities in the light of present knowledge.

Personal survival after death is only one aspect of eschatology. The whole phenomenon of apocalypticism takes up not only personal survival and judgement of the individual but the end of the world, cosmic cataclysm, final judgement of all living, new heavens and a new earth. The idea that all human history has followed a foreordained divine plan becomes an important theme in some apocalyptic literature. Apocalypticism, with its many facets, seems to have arisen in the Persian period, though its roots may go back to a variety of antecedents in Israel and the ancient Near East.

4.2 *Definition and Origins of Apocalypticism*

Defining apocalypticism is not easy. The term comes from the Greek words *apokaluptō,* 'to reveal', and *apokalupsis,* 'revelation', but has been especially influenced by the contents of such books as the New Testament book of Revelation. The characteristics and imagery of Revelation have often been those taken to be the constituents of apocalypticism, but there are also other books of antiquity which have 'apocalypse' in their titles. There is general agreement on a core of books which can be called apocalypses: Revelation, Daniel 7–12,1 Enoch, 2 Baruch, 4 Ezra. Within these are a number of characteristics which are widely found in apocalypses:

- Pseudepigraphical attribution
- Heavenly tour (other worldly journey)
- Revelation of divine secrets
- End of the world (cosmic cataclysm)
- Messianic figure
- Visions
- Other (angelic) worldly mediator
- Review of history (*ex eventu* prophecy)

The difficulty is deciding whether some characteristics are essential and some are not. What happens when you have one feature (e.g. a review of history) but not another (e.g. a heavenly journey)?

A great deal of effort has been made to define the literary genre of apocalypse; however, there is more to apocalypticism than apocalypses. Writings other than apocalypses may give us important information about apocalypticism. Therefore, we have to distinguish between the literary genre of apocalypse, which has to conform to certain formal criteria, and the phenomenon of apocalypticism whose characteristics are known from a variety of literary sources and religious and social manifestations. If we want to know about apocalypticism, we have to look at far more than just the strict apocalypses. Too often apocalypticism is discussed only as a literary entity when it can also be a social entity. It may be connected with social movements or social attitudes which go beyond a mere theoretical treatment in writing.

This is important to keep in mind, for those discussing apocalypticism have often assumed an automatic equation between literature and the social and religious aspects of the phenomenon. But this is not necessarily the case: 'apocalyptic communities' do not necessarily produce apocalypses. For example, Qumran has often been referred to as an apocalyptic community, yet it seems to have produced little in the way of apocalyptic literature in the strict sense. On the other hand, apocalyptic literature may be studied and believed by those who show no proclivity to form or live in an 'apocalyptic community'.

A lot of study has also gone into the question of the origin of apocalypticism, as if its origins will help us to understand it. They may indeed, but we should not assume so. Several origins have been suggested. The first of these is to make it a foreign borrowing, usually from Iran. The assumption is that during the Persian period apocalypticism grew up under Iranian influence. Not infrequently such a view has accompanied a rather negative attitude toward apocalypticism: if it is due to foreign influence, it can more easily be rejected as 'non-Israelite'. Of course, one should then ask why it was found so useful and attractive to have been borrowed into Israel!

Apart from this particular prejudice, another problem is trying to date the Iranian sources. Much Iranian literature is post-Islamic in its present form and thus a millennium or more later than the alleged borrowing by the Jews. To what extent the Iranian apocalyptic and related literature was already in existence, even in some earlier form, in the third or fourth century BCE is debatable. On the other hand, there are resemblances between the apocalyptic writings and some of the Akkadian literature which is unquestionably earlier than apocalypticism among the Jews. So the Near Eastern connection is definitely there, if perhaps to be somewhat differently conceived than some of the earlier arguments about Iranian borrowings.

As a second suggestion, some have noted the close relationship with prophecy and have argued that apocalypticism derives from prophecy. This approach is somewhat controversial because some scholars have wanted to privilege prophecy and disassociate apocalypticism from it. Others allow a connection but think apocalypticism is a degeneration of prophecy. Both of these approaches are rather negative towards apocalypticism, but others see it in a more positive light as simply a development of prophecy. They usually put an emphasis on apocalypticism as an Israelite phenomenon, though to use this to make it more acceptable is as fallacious an argument as to reject it because it is allegedly foreign. (I have argued that it should be classified as a sub-category of prophecy, but not everyone would agree with me.)

A third approach is to derive it from wisdom. This has not received a great deal of support because, despite having some resemblances to standard wisdom, apocalyptic literature is very different from books such as Proverbs. On the other hand, some biblical passages such as the book of Daniel and the Joseph story (Genesis 37, 39–50) have a good deal in common with both apocalypticism and wisdom. This has led to the thesis that apocalypticism is connected with wisdom but a version of wisdom somewhat different from that of Proverbs: *mantic* wisdom. This form of wisdom emphasizes intellect, learning, observation, thought, and divine guidance just as does Proverbs, but it has to do with knowledge of the future and the spiritual world – a form of esoteric wisdom.

Other proposals have been made from time to time, such as making it a scribal or a priestly phenomenon or associating it with the Hellenistic world. It looks as if there is some truth in these suggestions as well as the three general relationships noted above. The connection with prophecy is plain but so is that with mantic wisdom; this makes us realize the overlap between prophecy and mantic wisdom. In that sense, apocalypticism is a native development. Yet the probable influence from other ancient Near East cultures can also be taken as demonstrated. In recognizing this, one must not forget that the Hellenistic world inherited a great deal from its Near Eastern predecessors (see section 1.1.3), so that apocalypticism is a broad movement in the Hellenistic world and not confined to the Jews. The apocalyptic and related writings show scribal creation and nurture, but apocalypticism was probably also cultivated in some priestly circles, including most likely the Jerusalem priesthood. To understand the phenomenon, we have to be inclusive rather than exclusive.

4.3 Apocalypses and Related Literature

It is debated as to whether some of the prophetic books of the Old Testament already represent apocalypses. For example, a number of scholars would reckon that Zechariah 1–8 was already an apocalypse. Other Old Testament sections which have certain resemblances to apocalypses are Joel, Isaiah 24–27, and portions of Isaiah 56–66. The one Old Testament book which is universally counted as an apocalypse is Daniel 7–12. It is not, however, the earliest apocalypse by any means: this part of Daniel is no earlier than about 165 BCE.

Several sections of *1 Enoch* are probably a century or more older than this. The Astronomical Book is represented by 1 Enoch 72–82, but the present text of that book seems to be only a summary of its original contents; the Qumran fragments and some other comparative material indicate a much more extensive writing originally. The Astronomical Book is dated by some as early as the late fourth century, though it is not really in the form of an apocalypse. The Book of Watchers (*1 Enoch* 1–36), however, is an apocalypse and has been dated roughly to around 300 BCE. The Animal Apocalypse (85–90) is from roughly the time of Daniel 7–12, since it ends at the time of the Maccabaean revolt but before the temple was retaken; the

Dream Visions (83–84) are probably about the same time. The Epistle of Enoch (91–107) is now dated to the early first century BCE. There has been much recent controversy over the Parables (Similitudes) of Enoch (37–71), but many scholars want to date them to the first century CE. If so, they are the latest part of the book.

The *Testament of Abraham* seems to be from the first century CE. In it Abraham is able to witness the judgement of the souls of the dead. I would also consider the *Testament of Moses* to be an apocalypse, though not everyone would agree. A good deal of it is a review of history up to the time of Herod's sons. It is generally thought that an original version of it was written about the time of the Maccabaean revolt; this was later updated after the death of Herod the Great. The dating of *2 Enoch* is also controversial, but many would also see it as written during the first century CE.

Several apocalypses come from right at the end of the first century, about 100 CE. This would include the New Testament book of Revelation and also 4 Ezra (2 Esdras) and 2 Baruch. Some of the material of 4 Ezra and 2 Baruch is very similar, suggesting a close connection between these two books, but all three of these have some interesting points in common. Revelation is written from a Christian perspective, of course, even though it has much in common with Jewish apocalypses. Both 4 Ezra and 2 Baruch address the question of why the temple should be in ruins and the Jewish people in their present state of despair. The *Apocalypse of Abraham* is not easy to date, but many would see it as from roughly the same time as the other three apocalypses listed here.

4.4 Ideas about Life after Death

4.4.1 Introduction

As noted in section 4.1 most of the books of the Hebrew Bible do not seem to envisage life after death as such. Life in its proper sense ends at death, even if there is some shadowy vestige which continues to exist in Sheol. When belief in some form of afterlife began to enter Israelite thinking is not known. As indicated in section 4.1, the view that the dead could communicate with and influence the living may have been around in some parts of Israelite society from an early time, but this is a moot point. What is clear is that sometime in the Persian or early Greek period, ideas about the afterlife had entered Jewish thinking.

4.4.2 Resurrection of the Dead

It is sometimes asserted that the resurrection of the body was the characteristic Jewish belief. This is not borne out by the data. A variety of beliefs seem to be attested about the same time in Israelite history. One of these was the resurrection of the body, but there is little reason to think that it was earlier or more characteristic of Jewish thinking than the immortality of the soul or resurrection of the spirit. And it is clear that some Jews still maintained the older belief in no afterlife. The Sadducees (see section 2.7) are one group who thought so; so did Ben Sira. Writing about 190 BCE Ben Sira does not seem to think of any life beyond death, as interpreted by the vast majority of scholars. Therefore, it would be quite wrong to refer to any of these beliefs as 'characteristically' Jewish or *the* Jewish belief on the subject.

The earliest reference to the resurrection is probably found in the 'Isaiah Apocalypse' (Isaiah 24–27), though the dating of this passage is controversial. Here the resurrection of the dead into their previous bodily form seems to be in the mind of the author (26:19–21). Other passages of the Old Testament have been interpreted as references to the resurrection but probably did not have that original meaning. For example, Ezekiel 37 talks of the dry bones which become living human beings; however, it is clear that this is an allegory for the restoration of Israel (37:11–14), not a return of dead Israelites to life when only skeletons remained. Apart from Isaiah 24–27 which is difficult to date, the earliest datable reference to the resurrection is Daniel 12:2 from about 165 BCE. Here the resurrection is not universal but involves only some of the dead. The righteous achieve what is referred to as 'astral immortality'; that is, they become like the stars of heaven (12:3). After this resurrection is found widely in the literature.

A good example is 2 Maccabees 7 which describes the torture and death of a mother and her seven sons because they refused to break the law:

> [7:9] And when he was at his last breath, he said, 'You accursed wretch, you dismiss us from the present life, but the King of the universe will raise us up to an everlasting renewal of life, because we have died for his laws.' After him, the third was the victim of their sport. When it was demanded, he quickly put out his tongue and courageously stretched forth his hands [to be cut off], and said nobly, 'I got these from Heaven, and because of his laws I disdain them, and from him I hope to get them back again.'

This seems to expect the resurrection of the body, because the parts cut off would be restored. A clear example is found 2 Baruch 49–51:

> [50:2] For the earth will certainly then restore the dead it now receives so as to preserve them: it will make no changes in their form, but as it has received them, so it will restore them, and as I delivered them to it, so also will it raise them. For those who are then alive must be shown that the dead have come to life again, and that those who had departed have returned. And when they have recognized those they know now, then the judgement will begin, and what you have been told already will come to pass.

The exact form of the resurrection is not always specified, but we should not expect it always to entail resurrection of the body. Sometimes only the resurrection of the spirit is in mind, as in Jubilees 23:20–22:

> And at that time the Lord will heal his servants, and they shall be exalted and prosper greatly; and they shall drive out their adversaries. And the righteous shall see it and be thankful, and rejoice with joy for ever and ever; and they shall see all the punishments and curses that had been their lot falling on their enemies. And their bones shall rest in the earth, and their spirits shall have much joy; and they shall know that the Lord is one who executes judgement, and shows mercy to hundreds, and to tens of thousands, and to all that love him.

4.4.3 The Immortality of the Soul

Belief in the immortality of the soul is known at least as early as the Book of Watchers (*1 Enoch* 1–36). The souls of the various sorts of people are preserved in hollow places after death (*1 Enoch* 22):

> And from there I went to another place, and he showed me in the west a large and high mountain, and a hard rock and four beautiful places, and inside it was deep and wide and very smooth . . . Then Raphael, one of the holy angels who was with me, answered me and said to me, These beautiful places are intended for this, that the spirits, the souls of the dead, might be gathered into them; for them they were created, that here they might gather all the souls of the sons of men. And these places they made where they will keep them until the day of their judgement and until their appointed time – and that appointed time will be long – until the great judgement comes upon them.

As the rest of the passage indicates, the souls of the dead are already experiencing reward and punishment in their intermediate state. In this case, the existence of the soul after death seems to be combined with the idea of a final judgement. This may imply a general resurrection, though this is not stated explicitly. In other sections of *1 Enoch,* a resurrection is mentioned (46:6; 51:1; 90:33; 91:10; 92:3–4).

Other sources give no indication of a resurrection at all, only the immortal soul. A good example is Wisdom of Solomon which speaks of the soul (e.g., 3:1–9) but does not mention the resurrection. Whether Wisdom thinks the souls of all are immortal, or only those of the righteous, is debated. Many feel that immortality is not inherent in the soul itself but is a gift given only to the righteous.

The *Testament of Abraham* gives the clearest picture of how the souls are judged after death (Version A 11–14; Version B 9–11). The souls are brought before a throne on which Abel sits as judge. The one who presents the souls for judgement is Enoch, the scribe of righteousness (Version B only). The judged souls go either through the strait gate which leads to life (for the righteous) or the broad gate to destruction (for the sinners). Although there is a brief indication of belief in a general resurrection in the *Testament of Abraham* (Version B 7:16), judgement of each individual seems to take place immediately after death, and the emphasis is on this immediate judgement of the soul while the body rests in the grave.

On the other hand, the immortal souls and the resurrection may be combined, as in 2 Baruch 29–30:

> [30:2] And it shall come to pass at that time that the treasuries will be opened in which is preserved the number of the souls of the righteous, and they will come out, and the multitude of souls will appear together in one single assembly; and those who are first will rejoice, and those who are last will not be cast down. For each one of them will known that the predetermined end of the times has come. But the souls of the wicked, when they see all this, will be the more discomforted. For they will know that their torment is upon them and that their perdition has arrived.

4.5 Expectations for the End of the World

There was a widespread view that the age of the world was finite and that history was played out according to a predetermined divine plan. This is indicated by the 'review of history' found in many of the apocalypses and related writings. Many of these reviews seem to end just about the time the particular writing was written. It is not unusual for the review of history to follow biblical or known history fairly closely to the time of writing, then to make a genuine prediction at that point.

A good example is Daniel 11 in which the writer shows reasonable knowledge of the interaction between the Seleucid and Ptolemaic dynasties. At verse 40, however, the events described begin to differ from those known to us in historical accounts. The writer also mentions 'the time of the end'. The clear explanation is that the writer has been describing known history up to this point but then begins to engage in genuine prediction. Unfortunately, his predictions turned out to be wrong. Antiochus did not meet his end while camped in Palestine. Similar reviews of history – *vaticinia ex eventu* (prophecies after the event) – are found in the Animal Apocalypse (*1 Enoch* 85–90), the *Testament of Moses,* 2 Baruch 53–74, and the Apocalypse of Weeks (*1 Enoch* 93:2–9 + 91:12–17).

But whether or not there is a detailed review of history, the idea of the endtime and living near that time is found in many apocalypses. This is not always expressed in a clear-cut or definite manner, and in some cases the idea of the end of the world may have been only a vaguely expected and somewhat ill-defined belief. But one of the most characteristic elements of apocalyptic and related literature is the view that the eschaton has come, either for the individual or for the whole human race. For many, it was the world itself which was in its last days.

The most frequent way of expressing this was to see the present world empire, usually expressed under a symbol, as about to be destroyed. As already discussed above, Antiochus Epiphanes' Seleucid empire is represented in several passages in Daniel as a creature (7:19–27; 8:23–25), and is also represented as the King of the North in ch. 11. In each case, God himself intervenes to put an end to the final dominant kingdom. Another good example is the eagle vision of 4 Ezra 11–12 in which the Roman empire is symbolized by the eagle. After it is described at length, it is suddenly destroyed:

> [11:33] After this I looked again and saw the head in the middle suddenly disappear, just as the wings had done. But the two heads remained, which also in like manner ruled over the earth and its inhabitants. And while I looked, I saw the head on the right side devour the one on the left. Then I heard a voice saying to me, 'Look in front of you and consider what you see.' When I looked, I saw what seemed to be a lion roused from the forest, roaring; and I heard how it uttered a human voice to the eagle, and spoke . . . [12:1] While the lion was saying these words to the eagle, I looked and saw that the remaining head had disappeared. The two wings that had gone over to it rose up and set themselves up to reign, and their reign was brief and full of tumult. When I looked again, they were already vanishing. The whole body of the eagle was burned, and the earth was exceedingly terrified . . . [12:31] And as for the lion whom you saw rousing up out of the forest and roaring and speaking to the eagle and reproving him for his unrighteousness, and as for all his words that you have heard, this is the Messiah whom the Most High has kept until the end of days, who will arise from the offspring of David, and will come and speak with them. He will denounce them for their ungodliness and for their wickedness, and will display before them their contemptuous dealings. For first

he will bring them alive before his judgment seat, and when he has reproved them, then he will destroy them. But in mercy he will set free the remnant of my people, those who have been saved throughout my borders, and he will make them joyful until the end comes, the day of judgment, of which I spoke to you at the beginning.

A similar idea is found in the New Testament book of Revelation which is roughly contemporary with 4 Ezra. Rome is represented by a beast borrowed from Daniel (Revelation 13:1–4):

And I saw a beast rising out of the sea; and on its horns were ten diadems, and on its heads were blasphemous names. And the beast that I saw was like a leopard, its feet were like a bear's, and its mouth was like a lion's mouth. And the dragon gave it his power and his throne and great authority. One of its heads seemed to have received a death-blow, but its mortal wound had been healed. In amazement the whole earth followed the beast. They worshipped the dragon, for he had given his authority to the beast, and they worshipped the beast, saying 'Who is like the beast, and who can fight against it?'

Although this beast survives one mortal blow to the astonishment of the world, it is ultimately judged by the returning Christ and is 'thrown alive into the lake of fire that burns with sulphur' (Revelation 19:20).

One view was that the approaching endtime would be heralded by a series of 'troubles' (sometimes referred to as the 'Messianic woes' or 'birthpangs of the Messiah'). This is what the Olivet prophecy pictures in the Gospels (Mark 13; Matthew 24; Luke 21), as a brief quotation will show (Mark 13:8,19):

For nation will rise against nation, and kingdom against kingdom; there will be earthquakes in various places; there will be famines. This is but the beginning of the birthpangs . . . For in those days there will be suffering, such as has not been from the beginning of the creation that God created until now, no, and never will be. And if the Lord had not cut short those days, no one would be saved . . .

A similar picture is given in 4 Ezra 5:1–13:

Now concerning the signs: lo, the days are coming when those who inhabit the earth shall be seized with great terror, and the way of truth shall be hidden, and the land shall be barren of faith . . . [4]

and the sun shall suddenly begin to shine at night, and the moon during the day. Blood shall drip from wood, and the stone shall utter its voice; the peoples shall be troubled, and the stars shall fall. And one shall reign whom those who inhabit the earth do not expect, and the birds shall fly away together; and the Dead Sea shall cast up fish . . . [8] There shall be chaos also in many places, fire shall often break out, the wild animals shall roam beyond their haunts, and menstruous women shall bring forth monsters.

A further account of these signs is given in 4 Ezra 6; 18–28:

[20] When the seal is placed upon the age that is about to pass away, then I will show these signs: the books shall be opened before the face of the firmament, and all shall see my judgment together. Children a year old shall speak with their voices, and pregnant women shall give birth to premature children at three and four months, and these shall live and leap about . . . [24] At that time friends shall make war on friends like enemies, the earth and those who inhabit it shall be terrified, and the springs of the fountains shall stand still, so that for three hours they shall not flow.

A common theme in some of the classical historians (e.g. Herodotus) is that of 'prodigies' heralding important events – unusual or special happenings. In apocalypses these prodigies have their parallel in the signs preceding the endtime. A major feature of these 'woes' is the reversal of normality: the world is turned upside down; the expected order of society has become its opposite; nothing is the way it should be. Chaos has re-entered the cosmos. Yet even though these increase the suffering of mankind, they are welcome because God will soon intervene to bring an end to all human suffering. In some cases, the right-eous escape the endtime woes, but this does not always seem to be the case.

4.6 Calculating the Endtime

Many of the references to the endtime are non-specific, but they often make two assumptions: the endtime was predicted by God long ago, and the writers themselves are living in or near that time. Some texts go even further than this, however; they attempt to show that the time of the end had already been calculated according to a particular schema long before. When we look at different texts, we seem to find a different basis of calculation in different texts; in other words, a variety of modes or bases of calculation has been used. Most of these seem to arise from particular texts in the Old Testament, even if the texts used were rather obscure. Some of the modes used are discussed in the next two sections.

4.6.1 The Age of the World

Based on Psalm 90:4 the view developed that human history followed the plan of a thousand-year week. That is, all human history would be packed into 6000 years, followed by a millennial Sabbath. Exactly how early this developed is not clear. One of the earliest plain references to it is the early Christian writing *Epistle of Barnabas* from about 150 CE (15:4):

> Notice, children, what is the meaning of 'He made an end in six days.' He means this, that the Lord will make an end of everything in six thousand years, for a day with him means a thousand years.

However, the same idea seems to lie behind 2 Peter 3:8 and especially Revelation 20:

> [20:4] I also saw the souls of those who had been beheaded for their testimony to Jesus and to the word of God . . . They came to life and reigned with Christ a thousand years. (The rest of the dead did not come to life until the thousand years were ended.) This is the first resurrection. Blessed and holy are those who share in the first resurrection. Over these the second death has no power, but they will be priests of God and Christ, and they will reign with him a thousand years.

This model for human history then became quite widespread in early Christian writers, though in time there was a reaction against what was seen as too much emphasis on the physical 'indulgences' expected during the Millennium.

The question is how early the idea of a 'world week' arose in Judaism. Jubilees 4:30 has a statement similar to Psalm 90:4 but does not go further. From the first century the *Testament of*

Abraham presupposes a 7000-year programme of human history, though one version is clearer than the other:

> [Version A 19:7] And Death said, 'Hear, righteous Abraham, for seven ages I ravage the world and I lead everyone down into Hades – kings and rulers, rich and poor, slaves and free I send into the depth of Hades.'

> [Version B 7:15–16] And Michael said to Abraham, 'Your son Isaac has spoken the truth; for you are [the sun], and you will be taken up into the heavens, while your body remains on the earth until seven thousand ages are fulfilled.'

Josephus mentions that the earth was about 5000 years old in his own time (*Antiquities* Proem. 3 §13; *Against Apion* 1.1 §1). In 4 Ezra there is the puzzling figure of 5042 years to the time of Ezra (14:48 Syriac version). Although this has never been satisfactorily explained before, I believe that it is to be tied in with the Messianic Age of 400 years (4 Ezra 7:28). If we assume that the 5042 years is meant to refer to the real Ezra, this would make the writing of the book (c.100 CE) close to the year 5600. If we add the 400 years of the Messiah, this gives an age of the world of 6000 years before God then brings about the cosmic regeneration. If so, then the writer seems to have believed that he was living near the time of the coming of the Messiah. A number of Christian writers (e.g. Julius Africanus) put the birth of Jesus in the year 5500 from the creation of the world. This also seems to fit in with the idea that human history would run for 6000 years before 'God's time' would be introduced.

4.6.2 The Seventy-Weeks Prophecy

Daniel 9 has one of the most startling prophecies with a specific time frame. This passage explicitly asks about the prophecy of 70 years mentioned by Jeremiah (25:11–12; 29:10). It then goes on to reinterpret Jeremiah's prophecy as a reference to seventy *weeks* of years (Daniel 9:24–27). What is surprising is that more explicit reference is not made to this passage, especially to speculate on its meaning. It is normally taken to refer to the death of the high priest Onias III about 170 BCE just before the Maccabaean revolt (1.1.4), but it becomes important in later Christian writings as a way of calculating the coming of the Messiah. There is some evidence that speculation about it also occurred among Jewish interpreters, but the evidence is more circumstantial.

Perhaps one of the clearer and more interesting examples is found in the Qumran scrolls. The *Damascus Document* 1:5–11 speaks of a figure of 390 years. This of course corresponds with the period of Israel's punishment as stipulated in the book of Ezekiel (4:4–5), but this would not prevent the writer from also thinking of Daniel 9. The 390 years in the *Damascus Document* is followed by the figure of 20 years of groping until the Teacher of Righteousness comes. There are statements to the effect that a period of 40 years would elapse between the death of the Teacher and the end of the age (CD 20:14–15; 4QpPs^a 2:6–8). If one allows another round figure of 40 years (= one generation) for the life of the Teacher, we come to 490 years. The two figures of 40 years are stereotyped, but stereotyping is typical of this sort of chronographical speculation:

From Nebuchadnezzar to the first 'groping'	390
The period of 'groping' until the Teacher	20
The life of the Teacher	40
From the death of the Teacher to the endtime	40
Total	490

Two further interpretations may have the 70 weeks of Daniel as their base. In his description of the siege of Jerusalem, Josephus states (*War* 6.5.4 §311):

> Thus the Jews, after the demolition of Antonia [the fortress near the temple], reduced the temple to a square, although they had it recorded in their oracles that the city and the sanctuary would be taken when the temple should become four-square.

A second oracle is mentioned in the same context (*War* 6.5.4 §§312–13):

But what more than all else incited them to the war was an ambiguous oracle, likewise found in their sacred scriptures, to the effect that at that time one from their country would become ruler of the world. This they understood to mean someone of their own race, and many of their wise men went astray in their interpretation of it. The oracle, however, in reality signified the sovereignty of Vespasian, who was proclaimed Emperor on Jewish soil.

Both these oracles are somewhat unclear as to which biblical passage they refer. It is difficult to find one which seems to fit better than Daniel 9, however, which is why many scholars have connected one or both of these with the 70-weeks prophecy. This suggests that it was used as a means of trying to work out the end of the age in some circles, though the failure of such prophecies may have been the reason that clearer examples have not survived. One further example may be found in 11QMelchizedek which is quoted in the next section.

4.7 The Heavenly Messiah

As already noted in section 3.8, the concept of the Messiah primarily had to do with an earthly figure whose inspiration was either the Israelite king or high priest. Both were anointed figures. The idea of a heavenly figure as the Messiah is well known from the New Testament, but this was not the dominant view. Nevertheless, we have some texts which envisage a heavenly figure, though not always the same concept and certainly not corresponding to the New Testament figure. The New Testament figure was ultimately shaped by the Jesus tradition and, whatever the Jewish antecedents followed, took on its own unique configuration based on the Christological development within Christianity. It would not be surprising if the New Testament model differed from anything found in early Jewish texts.

One of the earliest texts with a heavenly Messiah is the text from Qumran called 11QMelchizedek (2:4–18):

[He said, *To proclaim liberty to the, captives* (Isa. lxi, 1). Its interpretation is that He] will assign them to the Sons of Heaven and to the inheritance of Melchizedek; f[or He will cast] their [lot] amid the po[rtions of Melchize]dek, who will return them there and will proclaim to them liberty, forgiving them [the wrong-doings] of all their iniquities.

And this thing will [occur] in the first week of the jubilee that follows the nine Jubilees. And the Day of Atonement is the e[nd of the] tenth [Ju]bilee, when all the Sons of [Light] and the men of the lot of Mel[chi]zedek will be atoned for. [And] a statute concerns them [to prov]ide them with their rewards. For this is the moment of the Year of Grace for Melchizedek. [And h]e will, by his strength, judge the holy ones of God, executing judgement as it is written . . . (Isa. lii, 7). Its interpretation; *the mountains* are the prophets . . . and *the messenger* is the Anointed one of the spirit, concerning whom Dan[iel] said, [. . .(Dan. ix, 25)]

The fragmentary nature of the text makes it difficult to interpret, but Melchizedek the Canaanite priest-king of Jerusalem in Genesis 14 has become a heavenly figure (identical with the archangel Michael) who opposes Satan. The deliverance comes at the end of ten jubilees (490 years), just as with Daniel 9. Indeed, Daniel 9:25 seems to be cited, though whether 'the Anointed one' is identical with Melchizedek or is a separate figure is not clear.

The Parables of Enoch (*1 Enoch* 37–71) also speak of a Messiah; a comparison of the various passages indicates that this Messiah is also identified with the figures called the 'Son of Man' and the 'Elect One' (cf. 45:3; 46:3; 48:2, 6; 49:2; 52:4; 53:6; 55:4). Eventually, this figure seems to be identified with Enoch himself, but that is thought by many to be a secondary development (71:14–17):

And that angel came to me, and greeted me with his voice, and said to me, You are the Son of Man who was born to righteousness, and righteousness remains over you, and the righteousness of the Head of Days will not leave you . . . And so there will be length of days with that Son of Man, and the righteous will have peace, and the righteous will have an upright way in the name of the Lord of Spirits for ever and ever.

Another text long known is from 4 Ezra 13. Although the term 'Messiah' is not used, a heavenly 'man from the sea', who is also referred to as God's 'son', has characteristics to take into account:

[13:3] As I kept looking the wind made something like the figure of a man come up out of the heart of the sea. And I saw that this man flew with the clouds of heaven; and wherever he turned his face to look, everything under his gaze trembled, and whenever his voice issued from his mouth, all who heard his voice melted as wax melts when it feels the fire . . . [13:25] This is the interpretation of the vision: As for your seeing a man come up from the heart of the sea, this is he whom the Most High has been keeping for many ages, who will himself deliver his creation; and he will direct those who are left . . . [13:51] I said, 'O sovereign Lord, explain this to me: Why did I see the man coming up from the heart of the sea?' He said to me, 'Just as no one can explore or know what is in the depths of the sea, so no one on earth can see my Son or those who are with him, except in the time of his day.'

4.8 Conclusions

Many treatments have emphasized eschatological expectations among the Jews of the late Second Temple period. This has been especially true among those for whom the study of Judaism has been ultimately an aid to understanding the New Testament. More recent research has recognized the variety of beliefs within Judaism of the time. Some Jews had strong eschatological interests; others evidently did not. We have to be careful about generalization. The diversity of belief is the one conclusion which emerges clearly from the data.

It is plain that *in some circles* apocalypticism was cultivated and/or eschatalogical speculations were important. Qumran was an example of the latter, though whether apocalypticism was important depends on how the term is defined. The existence of many Jewish apocalypses and related literature shows that there were people who were not only interested in such things but also (in some cases, at least) allowed these views to dominate their lives and thinking. Literature alone does not always tell how people actually applied such things in their daily lives, but we also have some reports of what people did about their beliefs.

When we look at eschatology in general, it is apparent that not all eschatological systems saw the endtime in apocalyptic terms. Some (for example, the book of Wisdom) seemed to see eschatology as only an individual matter – as what the person faced after death – without any expectations of a universal resurrection or other cosmic upheaval bringing this world to an end. Some believed in a resurrection of some sort, though there was not unanimity even on this point: some conceived of it in terms of a resurrection of the body, some as resurrection of the spirit, and often no details were given at all. Others believed in the immortality of the soul without any reference to a resurrection. Finally, a number of sources seem to combine belief in the immortal soul with a resurrection of some sort.

This interest in apocalypticism and eschatology could be a potent social force. Some believing in such things might well have a passivist attitude toward them: God would bring these about in his own good time, and his servants had only to stand and wait. But others saw their duty as active agents in the style of Phinehas who took direct measures to see that God's will was realized. Such attitudes lead to millenarian movements and to bloody revolts because nothing so motivates a mindset of self-sacrifice and refusal to compromise as the conviction that one is doing the will of God. Some of the revolutionary movements described in the previous chapter may well have had such religious ideology driving and underpinning them.

4.9 Guide to Further Reading

Views about the cult of the dead in Israel are discussed in Grabbe, *Priests, Prophets, Diviners, Sages*, 5.6 (pp. 141–45). The more detailed studies include

Bloch-Smith, Elizabeth, *Judahite Burial Practices and Beliefs about the Dead* (Journal for the Study of the Old Testament Supplements 123; JSOT/ASOR Monograph Series 7; Sheffield Academic Press, 1992).

Lewis, Theodore J. *Cults of the Dead in Ancient Israel and Ugarit* (Harvard Semitic Monographs 39; Atlanta: Scholars Press, 1989).

Schmidt, Brian B. *Israel's Beneficent Dead: Ancestor Cult and Necromancy in Ancient Israelite Religion and Tradition*

(Forschungen zum Alten Testament 11; Tübingen: Mohr Siebeck, 1994).

For general treatments of apocalypticism, see Grabbe, *Priests, Prophets, Diviners, Sages*, 6.5 (pp. 200-4), and the following:

Collins, John J. *The Apocalyptic Imagination: An Introduction to the Jewish Matrix of Christianity* (2nd edn, Grand Rapids, MI: Eerdmans, 1998).

Davies, Philip R. 'The Social World of the Apocalyptic Writings', in Ronald E. Clements (ed.), *The World of Ancient Israel: Sociological, Anthropological and Political Perspectives, Essays by Members of the Society for Old Testament Study* (Cambridge: Cambridge University Press, 1989), 251–71.

Grabbe, Lester L., and Robert D. Haak (eds), *Knowing the End from the Beginning: The Prophetic, the Apocalyptic, and their Relationships* (Journal for the Study of the Pseudepigrapha Supplements 46; London/New York: T & T Clark International, 2003).

Koch, Klaus, *The Rediscovery of Apocalyptic* (Studies in Biblical Theology, Second Series 22; London: SCM, 1970).

Lambert, W. G. *The Background of Jewish Apocalyptic* (Ethel M. Wood Lecture, University of London, 22 Feb. 1977; London: Athlone, 1978).

Rowland, Christopher, *The Open Heaven: A Study of Apocalyptic in Judaism and Early Christianity* (London: SPCK, 1982).

For a survey of apocalypses and related literature, as well as a discussion of the genre's definition, see:

Collins, John J. (ed.), *Apocalypse: The Morphology of a Genre* (Semeia 14; Atlanta: Scholars, 1979).

Further information on the literature mentioned here can be found in Nickelsburg, *Jewish Literature from the Bible to the Mishnah*; Stone, *Jewish Literature of the Second Temple Period*; Schürer/ Vermes, *History of the Jewish People*, vol. 3.

In addition to the discussion in Grabbe, *Judaic Religion in the Second Temple Period*, chs 12–13, the standard treatment about life after death and the various ways in which it was envisaged in early Judaism is:

> Nickelsburg, G. W. E. *Resurrection, Immortality, and Eternal Life in Intertestamental Judaism* (Harvard Theological Studies 26; Cambridge, MA: Harvard, 1972).

For a discussion of how the endtime was calculated, with bibliography to the time of writing, see:

> Grabbe, Lester L. 'Chronography in Hellenistic Jewish Historiography', *Society of Biblical Literature 1979 Seminar Papers* (ed. P. J. Achtemeier; Society of Biblical Literature Seminar Papers Series 17; Missoula, MT: Scholars, 1979) 2.43–68.
>
> — 'Chronography in 4 Ezra and 2 Baruch', *Society of Biblical Literature Seminar Papers 1981* (Society of Biblical Literature Abstracts and Seminar Papers; Chico: Scholars, 1981), 49–63.

On the 70-weeks prophecy of Daniel 9, see my article:

> Grabbe, Lester L. 'The 70-Weeks Prophecy (Daniel 9:24-27) in Early Jewish Interpretation', in Craig A. Evans and Shemaryahu Talmon (eds), *The Quest for Context and Meaning: Studies in Biblical Intertextuality in Honor of James A. Sanders* (Biblical Interpretation Series 28; Leiden: Brill, 1997), 595–611.

CHAPTER 5

INVERTED JUDAISM:
THE GNOSTIC CURRENT

5.1 Introduction

Some may be surprised to see Gnosticism associated with Judaism. The Gnostic texts often seem anti-Jewish, and many secondary treatments speak as if Gnosticism was plainly and simply a perversion of Christianity. Until this century, almost the only sources were the discussions in the Church Fathers. The problem was that these were hostile accounts. The patristic writers saw the Gnostics as a heresy which had broken away from Christianity, and their whole approach was to show how bad it was. Thus, they might be willing to repeat any slanders and derogatory reports without worrying too much about determining their accuracy. A similar group were the Manichaeans, a group to whom Augustine once belonged. The Manichaeans had many characteristics in common with earlier Gnostic groups and had certainly been influenced by Gnosticism.

Apart from a few texts found in the eighteenth century, it was primarily in the late nineteenth century and in the twentieth century that original Gnostic writings became available. It was also then that the one living Gnostic group, the Mandaeans, became known to scholars. It was these texts, written and used by Gnostic groups themselves, which allowed scholars finally to see their own thinking and beliefs and also to have a check on the patristic accounts. What was found included Gnostic texts which show Christian traits, Gnostic texts which show Jewish traits, and Gnostic texts which show Platonic connections. This has led many scholars to see Gnosticism as a religion in its own right but with various permutations – Christian, Jewish, 'pagan'.

The term 'gnostic' comes from the Greek word *gnōsis,* 'knowledge'. With a small initial letter, 'gnostic' is frequently used in reference to any system or tendency placing emphasis on knowledge as a way to salvation; the term is also often used loosely in discussion of various groups in New Testament writings. However, 'Gnostic' (often with an initial capital) is used in reference to a specific religious system with certain known characteristics. Most of the Gnostic systems known seem to have behind them a central Gnostic myth (discussed in section 5.3).

5.2 Gnostic Sources

The Mandaean and Manichaean sources are discussed in sections 5.4 and 5.5 below.

5.2.1 Nag Hammadi Codices

These were discovered in 1945 in southern Egypt, near the village of Faw Qibli in the region of the town of Nag Hammadi. The manuscripts are in Coptic and dated to the fourth century CE; however, they represent translations of earlier Greek writings. There are the remains of 13 codices with 52 separate writings, though some writings occur more than once in the manuscripts (e.g., the *Apocryphon of John* occurs three times and four others occur twice). Although most of the individual writings are Gnostic, not all of them are (they include, for example, Plato's *Republic, Sentences of Sextus, Teachings of Silvanus*).

The main writings of concern for our purposes are the *Apocryphon of John* (a 'Christian' writing – but the Christian elements seem confined to the framework and may well have been added to an earlier non-Christian work), *Apocalypse of Adam* (an apocalyptic work), and the *Hypostasis of the Archons* with its closely related work *On the Origin of the World.* Some other writings will also be mentioned below, but these four have many of the parallels with Jewish sources and Jewish interpretation to be discussed in section 5.6.

5.2.2 *Patristic Sources*

A number of patristic accounts are known, but many of these are dependent on one another and give little or no original material. Two sources which are particularly important are Irenaeus (c.130–200), who wrote a work *Adversus Haereses* (*Against Heresies*) which was widely copied and adapted by later writers, and Epiphanius (c.315–400) who wrote a treatise against the 'eighty heresies' called the *Panarion* (*Cure All*). Despite their obvious bias against Gnosticism, both of these writers had access to some original Gnostic writings and quote from them. The Nag Hammadi texts show the importance of both these sources for our understanding of Gnosticism.

5.3 *The Basic Gnostic Myth*

A Gnostic myth apparently lies at the base of the various Gnostic systems known to us. It is this myth which explains what humans are, where they came from, and how they may gain the state which is their ultimate goal. No one source describes this myth in detail; indeed, it is unlikely that there was ever one single version of it. A number of sources mention it in passing or mention various aspects of it. One description of it is found in Irenaeus, *Against Heresies* 1.29–31. Also, a fairly detailed version is found in the *Apocryphon of John* and in the *Hypostasis of the Archons*.

The myth as known looks very Neo-Platonic in that a single Monad or First Principle is the originator of all that is, and that the world is a series of emanations from this single unity who is God. The Monad produced a Second Principle known as Pronoia ('foreknowledge'), also known as Barbēlō, accompanied by a Pentad of Aeons. The name Barbelo is clearly not Greek, but its exact origin is still debated. It may be Semitic or even Egyptian. The next product is the Autogenes (the 'self-begotten'), identified with Christ in Christian Gnostic sources. The final level of the world of the Pleroma ('the entirety') are the 12 Aeons, one of whom is Pistis Sophia ('faithful wisdom').

Pistis Sophia committed a sin, however, overstepping her place in the order of things and thinking she could create without benefit of her consort or permission of the Monad. Her creation was an abortion, Chaos or Yaldabaōth the Demiurge or Chief Archon. Yaldabaoth is a Semitic name, probably from *yalda* ('child') and *bô'* ('come, go') (cf. *On the Origin of the World* 100:12–14) or possibly *yld* ('give birth, create') and Sabaoth. He is clearly the creator God of the OT but, in the inverted view of the Gnostic myth, he is not good but evil. His creation is the Archons, including Yao (Yahweh), Elouaiou (Eloah or Elohim), Adonin (Adonai?), Sabaoth – all names for the God of Israel in Jewish tradition – and 365 angels.

Yaldabaoth and the Archons together create the first man Adam. They do so by using as a model the reflected image of the Pleroma, but Adam has no strength and cannot rise. Sophia then allows a spark of spirit to them to give Adam vitality; in some versions Yaldabaoth breathes life into him. In so doing, Sophia tricks the Archons, because only then do they realize that Adam is actually superior to them. At this point, they seek to imprison him and take the spirit from him.

Redemption is by means of Zoe (Greek 'life', equivalent to Hebrew Eve/Hāwwāh whose name also means 'life'). She is the daughter of Pistis Sophia. It is she who comes down and invigorates Adam so that he can stand up. She also enters the Serpent and gives it wisdom (the serpent is good in the Gnostic myth), and she is the material Eve. Adam mates with this material Eve and produces Norea and Seth who give rise to the line of the Gnostics. But when Zoe leaves material Eve, the offspring is Cain, begotten by the Archons, from whose line come the non-Gnostics. The 365 angels mate with the women of the non-Gnostic line and also teach them unlawful things (parallel to Enoch, as discussed below in section 5.6).

Obviously, much of this myth is taken from Genesis, but Genesis turned on its head. What is good in Genesis is bad to the Gnostics, and what is bad is good. However, it is not just a case of having read Genesis and then making everything the opposite. On the contrary, many of the details of the myth

The Gnostic Myth (An Idealized Version)

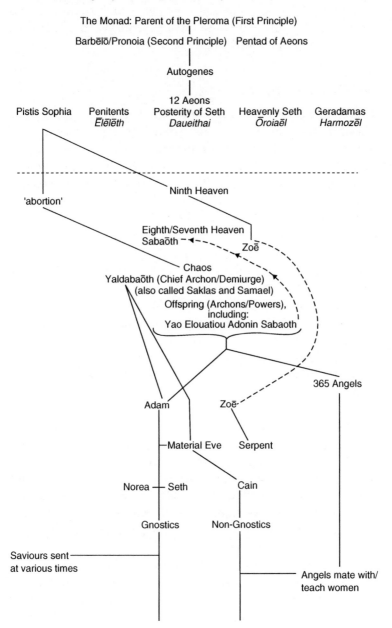

involve Jewish interpretations of the Old Testament text – interpretations which are likely to have been well known only to other Jews. It is likely that the myth as described above had its home in some branch of Judaism.

5.4 Manichaeans

The Manichaean sect was founded by Mani (216–77 CE), after whom it was named. Much has been learned in recent years because of the discovery of original Manichaean writings. Before that scholars had to depend on writings of Christian opponents. Although some of these (such as Augustine) were knowledgeable, they nevertheless had a strong bias against the Manichaeans and cannot be trusted to represent them fairly. The recently discovered 'Life of Mani' gives valuable information about Mani's early life and the origin of the group. We also have summaries of Manichaean belief from manuscripts found in many parts of the world. Mani had founded a missionary religion, and in addition to material from Persia where he did much of his work, writings have been found in central Asia, China, and Egypt.

Mani had spent part of his early life until the age of 24 in a Jewish-Christian baptismal sect. His religious system also has many Gnostic ideas and makes use of a version of the basic Gnostic myth outlined above. Whereas with other Gnostic groups we have writings but know little of how they actually lived their religion, with the Manichaeans we know how they put their beliefs into practice. They lived an ascetic lifestyle, eating no meat nor drinking alcohol. The inner circle (the Elect) eschewed sexual relations and did not even prepare their own food. They were cared for by the Auditors who were also vegetarian but were allowed to marry, though sexual relations were to be avoided as much as possible.

Mani included a number of books in his sacred canon, mainly his own original writings. However, he also incorporated a writing taken over from elsewhere: the *Book of Giants*. We now know from the Qumran writings that this was a Jewish book. The fragments preserved of the Manichaean book show that it was similar to the Qumran *Book of Giants*. Mani also evidently knew the Book of Watchers (*1 Enoch* 1–36).

5.5 Mandaeans

This is a small sect which has survived in Iraq and Iran. When it was first discovered, it was sometimes referred to as 'John Christians' because they looked to John the Baptist as their predecessor. It is neither Jewish nor Christian, though having some features in common with both. The adherents practice a regular ritual of baptism as an important cultic rite in sacred enclosures with running water called 'Jordans' (*yardana*) and are led by priests (though in recent years only one of the sacred enclosures is left and the rites may be done beside rivers).

A considerable debate has developed as to the origin of this group. It has been argued that it goes back to Palestine in the pre-70 period, but specialists disagree about how confident one can be about this view. For example, some take the connection with John the Baptist as a reliable tradition whereas others think it was a belief adopted only secondarily at a later time. Nevertheless, many specialists accept that the group originated in Palestine before 70 but later migrated to the Mesopotamian area (though the Mandaeans' own account of this has many legendary features). The sect itself is hostile to Judaism as such, but it has many Jewish elements and is likely to have had a Jewish origin. This view is in conformity with the thesis of an early Jewish proto-Gnosticism as discussed above.

The Mandaeans have a central religious myth which has much in common with the Gnostic myth outlined above. Their name comes from the root *yd'* and means 'knowers', and they seem to be the one Gnostic group surviving to modern times.

5.6 Examples of Jewish and Gnostic Parallels

5.6.1 Plays on Semitic Words

To the scholar of Jewish literature in Hebrew and Aramaic, a number of the names and other philological data leap out as evidence of a Jewish source. First, the name of the evil demiurge:

as already noted in section 5.3, Yaldabaoth looks Semitic even though the exact origin of the name is still debated. Samael ('blind god') has long been known from Jewish writings as a name for the chief of the demons. Saklas is probably from the Aramaic *sakla'* ('fool'). Other names are also Semitic and known from the Old Testament, as already noted: Yao (Yahweh), Elouaiou (Eloah or perhaps Elohim), Adonin/Adonaeia (Adonai?), Sabaoth.

A very interesting passage is found in slightly different versions in two writings. This concerns the coming of the serpent to Eve in the Garden of Eden:

> Then the female spiritual principle came [in] the snake, the instructor; and it taught [them] . . . (*Hypostasis of the Archons* 89:31–32)

> . . . whose mother the Hebrews call Eve of Life, namely, the female instructor of life. Her offspring is the creature that is lord. Afterwards, the authorities called it 'Beast' . . . The interpretation of 'the beast' is 'the instructor.' For it was found to be the wisest of all beings. (*On the Origin of the World* 113:32–114:4)

What we have here is a four-fold play on words in Hebrew or Aramaic: חוא – which is both the proper name Eve and also means 'life' and 'animal/beast'; חויא – serpent; מחוא – instructor.

5.6.2 *The Myth of the Fallen Angels*

An old myth in Judaism is the story of the union of angels with human women. The base text is Genesis 6:1–4, but the full-blown story is found primarily in *1 Enoch* 6–9 (cf. also *Jubilees* 5:1–7) and in the *Book of Giants* known from Qumran. The question of whether the myth is an interpretation of Genesis 6 or whether Genesis 6 represents a brief reflection of the myth is debated. Here are portions of the main account of the legend in *1 Enoch* 6–9:

> And it came to pass, when the sons of men had increased, that in those days there were born to them fair and beautiful daughters. And the angels, the sons of heaven, saw them and desired them. And they said to one another, Come, let us choose for ourselves

wives from the children of men, and let us beget for ourselves children. And Semyaza [Shemihazah], who was their leader, said to them, I fear that you may not wish this deed to be done, and that I alone will pay for this great sin. And they all answered him and said, Let us all swear an oath, and bind one another with curses not to alter this, but to carry out this plan effectively . . . And they took wives for themselves, and everyone chose for himself one each. And they began to go into them and were promiscuous with them. And they taught them charms and spells, and showed to them the cutting of roots and trees. And they became pregnant and bore large giants, and their height was three thousand cubits. These devoured all the toil of men, until men were unable to sustain them . . . And Azazel [Asael] taught men to make swords, and daggers, and shields and breastplates. And he showed them the things after these, and the art of making them: bracelets, and ornaments, and the art of making up the eyes and of beautifying the eyelids, and the most precious and choice stones, and all kinds of coloured dyes. And the world was changed.

Several elements within this story are represented in the Gnostic texts: the plan or conspiracy of the angels, cohabitation of the angels with human women, the production of offspring, the motif of metals (*Apocryphon of John* 29.17–30.10; cf. *Origin of the World* 123:4–13):

And he made a plan with his powers. He sent his angels to the daughters of men, that they might take some of them for themselves and raise offspring for their enjoyment. And at first they did not succeed. When they had no success, they gathered together again and they made a plan together. They created a counterfeit spirit, who resembles the Spirit who had descended, so as to pollute the souls through it. And the angels changed themselves in their likeness into the likeness of their [the daughters of men's] mates, filling them with the spirit of darkness, which they had mixed for them, and with evil. They brought gold and silver and a gift and copper and iron and metal and all kinds of things. And they steered the people who had followed them into great troubles, by leading them astray with many deceptions.

A play on the wording of Genesis 6:4 is also evident. The Hebrew text has *hannĕfilîm*, which is usually taken from the root *npl*, 'to fall'. The *nefilim* are certainly the 'fallen ones', both in the

Enochic myth of the fallen angels and in the Gnostic text. The word also gets interpreted as 'giants', though how this happens is not clear. But another meaning of the word is 'abortion', and this finds clear expression in the Gnostic texts where the off-spring of Pistis Sophia is the misshapen abortion Yaldabaoth (*Hypostasis of the Archons* 94:15; cf. *Apocryphon of John* 10:1–9).

The relationship between the Enoch and the Gnostic myths is not a simple one. The fallen angel leaders Asael and Shemihazah seem in some respects at least to be the equivalent of the Demiurge. In the various forms of the tradition, the fallen angels are cast into Tartarus or the equivalent as a part of their punishment:

> For if God did not spare the angels when they sinned, but cast them into hell [Tartarus] and committed them to chains of deepest dark-ness to be kept until the judgment . . . (2 Peter 2:4)

> And further the Lord said to Raphael, Bind Azazel [Asael] by his hands and his feet, and throw him into the darkness. And split open the desert which is in Dudael, and throw him there. And throw on him jagged and sharp stones, and cover him with darkness; and let him stay there for ever, and cover his face, that he may not see light, and that on the great day of judgement he may be hurled into the fire . . . And the Lord said to Michael, Go, inform Semyaza [Shemihazah] and the others with him who have associated with the women to corrupt themselves with them in all their uncleanness. When all their sons kill each other, and when they see the destruc-tion of their beloved ones, bind them for seventy generations under the hills of the earth until the day of their judgement . . . (*1 Enoch* 10:4–13)

Similarly, Yaldabaoth is cast into Tartarus (*Hypostasis of the Archons* 95:10–35):

> And he [Yaldabaoth] said to his offspring, 'It is I who am the god of the entirety.' And Zoe (Life), the daughter of Pistis Sophia, cried out and said to him, 'You are mistaken, Sakla!' – for which the alter-nate name is Yaltabaoth. She breathed into his face, and her breath became a fiery angel for her; and that angel bound Yaldabaoth and cast him down into Tartaros below the abyss.

The repentance of Sabaoth is a feature of some versions of the Gnostic myth, as already described above (*Hypostasis of the*

Archons 95:13–96:3; cf. *On the Origin of the World* 103:32–107:14).
It comes just after the description of Yaldabaoth's being cast
into Tartarus:

> Now when his offspring Sabaoth saw the force of that angel, he
> repented and condemned his father and his mother matter. He
> loathed her, but he sang songs of praise up to Sophia and her
> daughter Zoe. And Sophia and Zoe caught him up and gave him
> charge of the seventh heaven, below the veil between above and
> below. And he is called 'God of the Forces, Sabaoth,' since he is up
> above the forces of chaos, for Sophia established him. Now when
> these [events] had come to pass, he made himself a huge four-faced
> chariot of cherubim, and infinitely many angels to act as ministers,
> and also harps and lyres. And Sophia took her daughter Zoe and
> had her sit upon his right to teach him about the things that exist in
> the eighth [heaven]; and the angel [of] wrath she placed upon his
> left. [Since] that day, [his right] has been called life; and the left has
> come to represent the unrighteousness of the realm of absolute
> power above.

It should be noted that in the basic Gnostic myth the God of
the Old Testament is essentially split into two, the supreme first
principle of the Pleroma and the wicked Demiurge. Then, in
this story of the repentance of Sabaoth, a further splitting takes
place. Now the God of the Old Testament (ignorant and wicked
in the Gnostic view) is further split into a repentant and par-
tially exalted being in the seventh heaven, similar to the picture
in Ezekiel, and the ignorant wicked creator.

According to the mediaeval *Midrash of Shemhazai*, which prob-
ably has its origin in a much earlier Enoch tradition, Shemhazai
(Shemihazah) repents of his deeds (quoted from Milik, *Books of
Enoch*, p. 328):

> When they [the sons of Šemḥazai] awoke from their sleep they
> arose in confusion, and, going to their father, they related to him
> the dreams. He said to them: 'The Holy One is about to bring
> a flood upon the world, and to destroy it, so that there will remain
> but one man and his three sons.' . . . What did Šemḥazai do? He
> repented and suspended himself between heaven and earth head
> downwards and feet upwards, because he was not allowed to open
> his mouth before the Holy One – Blessed be He – , and he still
> hangs between heaven and earth.

5.6.3 The Garden of Eden

The Gnostic myth has a great deal taken from the Garden of Eden episode of Genesis, some points of which have already been noted; there is no need to repeat what has already been described, but this section can fill out the picture with some additional details.

One of the basic points of the Gnostic myth concerns the creation of Adam by the Archons rather than by the true God. Jewish sources of course have Adam ultimately the product of God, but Philo for one has him created by angels at God's direction (*Fuga* 68–70). There is also a late tradition that Adam was only a *golem* (clay man) at creation until God breathed in the breath of life (*Genesis Rabbah* 14:8). This has an interesting parallel to the Gnostic story, but the *Genesis Rabbah* is probably from the fourth century CE and thus rather late.

The Nag Hammadi *Apocalypse of Adam* seems to be a non-Christian text (though the matter is still debated). This has clear Gnostic features, but certain sections show remarkable resemblances to the Adam and Eve tradition as found in the Jewish *Life of Adam and Eve* in Latin and the Greek *Apocalypse of Moses*. In the first part of both accounts, Adam gives a revelation to his son Seth in the form of a testament (*Apocalypse of Adam* 64:1–19; 85:19–31; *Life of Adam and Eve* 25–29; 51:3). In the Gnostic myth Adam and Eve are persecuted by the ignorant Demiurge who is actually inferior to them (*Apocalypse of Adam* 66:14–67:14); this has close parallels to Satan's own story of his expulsion from heaven (*Life of Adam and Eve* 12–16). Both accounts tell of coming destruction both by water and by fire (*Apocalypse of Adam* 69:2–76:7; *Life of Adam and Eve* 49:2–3). Finally, in both versions Seth is instructed to write these things down on stone (tablets or on a mountain) which would survive the Flood and be available to be read by later generations (*Apocalypse of Adam* 85:2–17; *Life of Adam and Eve* 50–51). This has led some scholars to argue that a common 'Testament of Adam' lies behind both the Gnostic and the Jewish work.

A midrash on the serpent is found in several Gnostic accounts (*Origin of the World* 113:21–114:4; 118:16–120:16; *Testimony of Truth* 45:30–46:1). This takes the details as known from Genesis

3–4 but with a Gnostic twist. The serpent is in fact the 'instructor', created by Sophia to bring enlightenment to the Gnostic
race. He is wise and teaches knowledge to Eve. 'God' (Yaldabaoth and the Archons) curses the serpent (without effect) and
also Adam and Eve because they now have an advantage over
the Archons. The episode illustrates the ignorance and malice
of this 'God' because he envies the knowledge Adam gains by
eating of the tree and punishes him. He is also blind because he
has to question Adam about what he has done and was not able
to foresee what Adam would do.

According to some of the Gnostic sources, Cain was the offspring of Eve and Samael (*Hypostasis of the Archons* 89:17–28; *On
the Origin of the World* 116:13–19). A similar interpretation of
Genesis, in which Cain is a product of Eve and Satan, can be
found in a number of Jewish sources, though unfortunately
most of these are quite late (e.g. Targum Pseudo-Jonathan on
Genesis 4:1 and 5:3; *Pirke de Rav Eliezer* 21).

5.6.4 Other Parallels

The figure of Sophia is quite important to the core Gnostic
myth. Her name is the Greek word for 'wisdom'. Within Jewish
sources, there is a long history of speculation on the figure of
wisdom, already beginning with Proverbs 1–9 (the dating of this
section of Proverbs is still controversial). Wisdom became out-
wardly pictured as almost a goddess figure – as one who was
separate from but alongside God. She was ultimately seen as
simply a personification of God's mind or other characteristic(s)
of his, but the language used of her is to make her a divine figure in her own right. In some Jewish sources (e.g. in Philo), this
figure is the Logos; in others it is Wisdom. This all creates a certain amount of tension, but the long tradition of Jewish speculation on the figure of Wisdom clearly lies behind Sophia in the
Gnostic myth.

The treatise known as *Zostrianos* seems to take its name from
the Persian prophet Zoroaster (Zarathushtra). Although very
much damaged, the treatise seems to describe a heavenly ascent
of Zostrianos. There are many parallels with the Jewish book
of *2 Enoch* in which Enoch rises through a variety of heavens

(the two versions of *2 Enoch* have a different number of heavens). A similar comparison can be made between *2 Enoch* and the Corpus Hermeticum tractate 1 known as *Poimandres*. This last is a revelation about creation from Poimandres who is the Intellect of the Realm of Absolute Power. *Poimandres* has parallels with Gnostic writings, especially its dualism between intellect and body, between spirit and matter, and it has both the supreme intellect and a lower Demiurge. On the other hand, it does not have the hostility towards the creator found in Gnosticism generally. The writer has clearly drawn on the book of Genesis for his account of creation; indeed, it has many resemblances to Philo's account in his *Opificio Mundi*.

A Jewish tradition developed around Solomon that he was an exorcist and a master of demons. This is already found as early as Josephus (*Antiquities* 8.2.5 §45):

> And God granted him knowledge of the art used against demons for the benefit and healing of men. He also composed incantations by which illnesses are relieved, and left behind forms of exorcisms with which those possessed by demons drive them out, never to return.

This tradition is given elaborate testimony in the *Testament of Solomon* from the early centuries CE in which Solomon harnesses the demons for the building of the temple, as well as imprisoning some within it:

> When I heard these things, I, Solomon, got up from my throne and saw the demon shuddering and trembling with fear. I said to him, 'Who are you? What is your name?' The demon replied, 'I am called Ornias.' . . . After I sealed [the demon] with my seal, I ordered him into the stone quarry to cut for the Temple stones which had been transported by way of the Arabian Sea and dumped along the seashore. (2:1–5)

> Then I ordered him [the demon Kunopegos] to be cast into a broad, flat bowl, and ten receptacles of seawater to be poured over [it]. I fortified the top side all around with marble and I unfolded and spread asphalt, pitch, and hemp rope around over the mouth of the vessel. When I had sealed it with the ring, I ordered [it] to be stored away in the Temple of God. (16:6–7)

This extra-biblical tradition is also known by the author of the *Testimony of Truth* (69:32–70:24):

> Some of them fall away [to the worship of] idols. [Others] have [demons] dwelling with them [as did] David the king. He is the one who laid the foundation of Jerusalem; and his son Solomon, whom he begat in [adultery], is the one who built Jerusalem by means of the demons, because he received [power]. When he [had finished building, he imprisoned] the demons [in the temple]. He [placed them] into seven [waterpots. They remained] a long [time in] the [waterpots], abandoned [there]. When the Romans [went] up to [Jerusalem] they discovered [the] waterpots, [and immediately] the [demons] ran out of the waterpots as those who escape from prison. And the waterpots [remained] pure [thereafter]. [And] since those days, [they dwell] with men who are [in] ignorance, and [they have remained upon] the earth.

5.7 Conclusions

This chapter has been the most speculative of the four currents in Judaism. Was there really a 'gnostic' current in Judaism? Many scholars feel that the examples noted above prove that there was a Jewish form of Gnosticism or at least proto-Gnosticism at one time. The main problem is that Gnosticism seems anti-Jewish. We must keep in mind, however, that Christianity became anti-Jewish even though it clearly originated in Judaism. To get from Judaism to Gnosticism is not easy, but it is certainly not impossible. Various aspects of Gnosticism already have their parallels in known forms of Judaism. One does not have to bridge the gap all in one go.

The clearest connections are found with the book of Genesis, but it is not just the Genesis of the Old Testament text. It is, rather, a Genesis interpreted. It is a Genesis expanded and developed by a long period of speculation, commentary, and growth of tradition. This form of the Genesis story is not likely to have been easily accessible to non Jews. The best explanation seems to be that it originated in a form of Jewish Gnosticism or proto-Gnosticism.

More difficult is the claim that this Jewish Gnosticism was a pre-Christian Gnosticism. What is non-Christian is not necessarily pre-Christian. On the other hand, we find Gnosticism already well attested in the second century CE. Also, the situation in Judaism after 70 was not conducive to this sort of development; it seems likely that any Jewish proto-Gnosticism was already in existence before the 66–70 war.

What this chapter has helped demonstrate is the complexity of Judaism before 70. In addition to Gnosticism, one could go into such matters as magic and the other esoteric arts (astrology, divination, necromancy, and the like) which were also aspects of Judaism of the time, but that would require another full study. A proper understanding of Jewish religion and culture requires that all these things be taken into account. Again, it demonstrates how wrong-headed is the image that so many people work with, which is that of the modern Orthodox or even Hasidic forms of Judaism. On the contrary, modern Judaism itself is not monolithic (secular, Conservative, and Reform Jews far outnumber the Orthodox, and the Hasidic movement is in fact very small), and modern Judaism is in any case a centuries-long development. Many of the pre-70 strands of Judaism were cut off by the 66–70 war or disappeared soon afterwards because of the changed circumstances. Others developed in their own way, leading away from Judaism itself: the Christians and perhaps the Gnostics. The mystical, magical, and other currents also continued and flourished alongside the developing rabbinic Judaism, though primarily underground.

5.8 Guide to Further Reading

For a translation of the main Gnostic texts, see:

> Robinson, James M. (ed.), *The Nag Hammadi Library in English* (San Francisco: Harper, revised edition, 1989).

> Layton, Bentley. *The Gnostic Scriptures: A New Translation with Annotations and Introductions* (London: SCM, 1987).

For a general introduction to Gnosticism, see Layton, *The Gnostic Scriptures*, and:

Rudolph, K. *Gnosis: the Nature and History of an Ancient Religion* (Edinburgh: T. & T. Clark, 1983).

Filoramo, Giovanni. *A History of Gnosticism* (translator A. Alcock; Oxford: Blackwell, 1992).

On the question of Judaism and Gnosticism, see Grabbe, *Judaism from Cyrus to Hadrian*, especially 8.2.13 (pp. 514–19), and

Pearson, B. A. 'Jewish Sources in Gnostic Literature', in Michael E. Stone (ed.), *Jewish Writings of the Second Temple Period* (Compendia rerum iudaicarum ad Novum Testamentum 2/2; Minneapolis, MN: Fortress, 1984), 443–81.

Fallon, Francis T. *The Enthronement of Sabaoth: Jewish Elements in Gnostic Creation Myths* (Nag Hammadi Studies 10; Leiden: Brill, 1978).

Reeves, John C. *Heralds of that Good Realm. Syro-Mesopotamian Gnosis and Jewish Traditions* (Nag Hammadi and Manichaean Studies 41; Leiden: Brill, 1996).

Stroumsa, Gedaliahu A. G. *Another Seed: Studies in Gnostic Mythology* (Nag Hammadi Studies 24; Leiden: Brill, 1984).

On the Mandaeans and Manichaeans, a selection of texts in English translation is found in:

Haardt, Robert. *Gnosis: Character and Testimony* (Leiden: Brill, 1971).

Foerster, Werner. *Gnosis: A Selection of Gnostic Texts II. Coptic and Mandaean Sources* (Oxford: Clarendon, 1974).

Part of the Life of Mani has been translated into English, as has been one of the main Manichaean texts:

Cameron, R., and A. J. Dewey. *The Cologne Mani Codex* (*P. Colon. inv. nr. 4780*)*: 'Concerning the Origin of his Body'*

(Society of Biblical Literature Texts and Translations 15; Early Christian Literature 3; Atlanta: Scholars, 1979).

Gardner, Iain. *The Kephalaia of the Teacher. The Edited Coptic Manichaean Texts in Translation with Commentary* (Nag Hammadi and Manichaean Studies 37; Leiden: Brill, 1995).

On the Manichaeans, the standard treatments are:

Lieu, Samuel N. C. *Manichaeism in the Later Roman Empire and Medieval China* (2nd edn; Wissenschaftliche Untersuchungen zum Neuen Testament 63; Tübingen: Mohr, 1992).

— *Manichaeism in Mesopotamia and the Roman East* (Religions in the Graeco-Roman World 118; Leiden: Brill, 1994).

— *Manichaeism in Central Asia and China* (Nag Hammadi and Manichaean Studies 45; Leiden: Brill, 1998).

For an introduction to the Mandaeans, see Rudolph, *Gnosis*, ch. , and his preface to the translated texts in Foerster. See also the following, which includes a number of central texts in translation:

Lupieri, Edmondo, *The Mandaeans: The Last Gnostics* (transl. Charles Hindley; Italian Texts and Studies on Religion and Society; Grand Rapids, MI: Eerdmans, 2002).

A translation of the main Jewish texts mentioned here can be found in Sparks (ed.), *Apocryphal Old Testament*, and Charlesworth (ed.), *Old Testament Pseudepigrapha*. The Qumran fragments of Enoch and the Book of Giants are discussed in the following book (which also gives the text and translation of the medieval Midrash of Shemihazai [pp. 322–29]):

Milik, J. T. *The Books of Enoch: Aramaic Fragments of Qumran Cave 4* (Oxford: Clarendon, 1976).

The main commentary on much of *1 Enoch* is the following (a second volume is in preparation):

Nickelsburg, George W. E. *1 Enoch 1: A Commentary on the Book of 1 Enoch, Chapters 1–36, 81–108* (Hermeneia; Minneapolis, MN: Fortress, 2001).

A comparison of the Qumran and Manichaean Book of Giants is given by:

Reeves, John C. *Jewish Lore in Manichaean Cosmogony: Studies in the* Book of Giants *Traditions* (Monographs of the Hebrew Union College 14; Cincinnati, OH: Hebrew Union College Press, 1992).

The main arguments against pre-Christian Gnosticism are found in:

Yamauchi, Edwin M. *Pre-Christian Gnosticism: A Survey of the Proposed Evidences* (Grand Rapids, MI: Eerdmans, 1973).

CHAPTER 6

⟨>∞∞<⟩

SUMMARY AND CONCLUSIONS

The previous chapters have considered a variety of religious currents in Judaism before 70 of the Common Era. The metaphor of 'current' is useful because it suggests several features about the Jewish religion of the time which we need to ponder at greater length. Currents refer to smaller fluxes and flows in a broad stream of water. In a stream or river, many different currents can be found. Some will form a part of the general movement of the mass of waters, but there will also be currents independent of that flow, perhaps forming eddies or even cross-currents which impede or redirect the main flow. A current may flow separately for a time, then join with another current or currents to form a unity for a while but then branch off once again to go its own way.

Similarly, when applied to electricity, a current may complicate the whole. A flash of lightning has a core of electric current which flows from a negative source to a positive one. Yet this flow is not in a straight line, as one might expect, but follows a crooked and devious path, going first one direction then another before finally reaching its goal. That destination is not necessarily foreordained, however, since there are various positive poles attracting the negative charge. Speed photography has shown that many partial branches radiate off the main path of the current, showing attractions from other sources which never complete the circuit. In some cases, though, the current splits up and connects with more than one positively charged object.

So the implications of using 'current' are those of diversity, interaction, and movement. An expression which became popular some years ago in biblical studies was 'trajectory'. This implied a similar picture. Rather than thinking of a static entity, called Christianity or Judaism, with the odd heresy splitting off at the edges, the phenomenon was seen as made up of a set of many moving parts, each following its own path but influenced by the paths of other movements contemporary with it. The picture of Judaism as a monolith or 'orthodoxy' or church is belied by the enormous diversity evidenced by the many movements at the time. My subject is Judaism, of course, but it is important to be aware that recent studies in early Christianity also envisage a similar state of affairs.

None of the currents described here constitutes the Judaism of that time, any more than a single current makes up the entire stream. Each of the currents formed an important element within first-century Judaism; each was a constituent of the whole. But they also flowed, collided, eddied, and ebbed – intermixing, joining, dividing – in a whirling confused mass of constantly changing movement. It is this, rather the common image of a static 'orthodoxy' with a few deviant elements, which represents the Judaism in the time of Hillel, Jesus, and Herod. Judaism at the turn of the era was a pluralistic, multi-faceted entity with great diversity and complexity.

Each of the currents described here – textual, revolutionary, apocalyptic, Gnostic – represents a single moving force in the Jewish society of Palestine at that time, but this does not mean that each was separate and distinct. On the contrary, an individual might belong to more than one stream. The currents overlapped and complemented each other in some cases; in other cases, they opposed one another and collisions between them produced great turbulence in society. These currents are not, in general, to be identified with specific sects.

These religious and social streams have a long history. If we ignore the period of the monarchy, which is a separate study in itself, we can already see divisions within the Jewish community as early as the beginning of the Persian period. Although the reliability of the information in the book of Ezra is debated, some of the issues in it are paralleled in the book of Nehemiah; together they already suggest differences of opinion in the

Jewish community on some major issues. One important issue was the relationship between the Jewish community and the outside world. The books of Ezra and Nehemiah exhibit a certain xenophobia, whereas some members of the community wished to embrace the surrounding culture. Some – including various priests – went so far as to marry outside the community.

This might give the impression that this 'pious' stance was the standard one, but subsequent history shows that this was not at all the case. The book of Nehemiah itself indicates that there were many Jewish leaders who were willing to work with Nehemiah but also saw no reason to cut their friendly relationship with Tobiah (cf. Neh. 6.17–19). The breaking up of legitimate marriages – many of them probably involving wives from among the Jewish population that had not been deported – would not have gone down well. In the following centuries the Tobiad family continued to be important and respected in the region. We also have evidence that many Jews were not adverse to establishing contacts with the outside world – indeed, that such contacts were unavoidable, in any case. The vision of the Jewish community in Ezra and Nehemiah was not the one that prevailed in the short term.

The apocalyptic stream may also have its roots in the Persian period. Some have seen evidence of it in the literature of such books as Zechariah and Third Isaiah (Isaiah 56–66). Certainly Zechariah 1–8 is very similar to later apocalyptic literature, and many would classify it as an apocalypse. There are cogent arguments that prophecy had a strong input into apocalypticism. Even if full-blown apocalypticism had not developed already in the Persian period, most would be comfortable at least with the term proto-apocalyptic. Although scholars have long distinguished apocalyptic from prophecy, it can be argued that there is a close relationship: many of the characteristics of prophecy can be found in apocalyptic writings and vice versa. In both cases, the intent is to communicate God's will – often obtained by special revelation – to the reader.

Judaism is often seen in terms of the various sects – the Pharisees, Sadducees, and Essenes. Although this way of understanding the religion is misconceived, these sects were important. Josephus, the source of most information on the sects, first mentions them during the Hasmonaean period. If their roots go back earlier, we are not told so. However, some have argued that the Qumran community begins its history already in the early post-exilic period, though this is a disputed issue.

Thus, regardless of the precise origins of the sects, the diversity demonstrated in the preceding chapters has a long history. As noted in Chapter 2, the three main sects (according to Josephus' reconstruction) were all a part of textual Judaism. The Sadducees, Pharisees, and Essenes all three gave weight to the written Torah and made use of the scribal skills of study, interpretation, and composition. Each had absorbed a good deal from the wisdom stream which flowed from ancient Israel to rabbinic literature, picking and choosing those elements which they found compatible and useful or perhaps just unconsciously assimilating them as time went on.

It would be a mistake to see Judaism as only a religion of the written books which became canonical as the Hebrew Bible or the Old Testament, as is sometimes assumed, because each element within this assumption is problematic. First of all, Judaism could not become a 'religion of the book' until the books were edited or written and then became accepted as authoritative. Instead, Judaism began as and remained a *temple religion* until the temple was destroyed for good in 70. The cult was the main form of worship, and for Jews in Palestine within relatively easy reach of Jerusalem to neglect worship at the temple would have been regarded as a grave omission.

Secondly, the canon as we think of it was not in existence before 70. Many or perhaps all of the books which went to make up the later Jewish canon were already extant and most of them had become authoritative in some sense to many Jews. Nevertheless, we have no evidence that the later Hebrew canon was accepted as a standard. The Qumran community apparently accepted a variety of sacred books beyond those of the Old Testament and also did not use some in our present Hebrew Bible (e.g. Esther); other Jewish communities (e.g. Alexandria) may have had a different estimate of the various biblical books. Even in rabbinic literature there is discussion of such books as Ecclesiastes and the Song of Songs.

Yet sacred writings developed and became increasingly important as time went on. With the acceptance of some literature as
having special character came the practice of interpretation
and exegesis. We have many examples of the use of literature as
the source of authority and inspiration and as having a message
for the contemporary generation. It has been proposed that
examples of interbiblical exegesis are already found within the
biblical text. Although many of these are debatable, Daniel 9
clearly refers to Jeremiah. Likewise, Ben Sira draws heavily on
traditions which seem to correspond closely to our present biblical text much of the time (though he does not know about
Ezra and Daniel, for example). It is when we come to Qumran
that we find many examples of commentaries on biblical passages. Similarly, in first-century Alexandria, Philo comments on
large sections of Genesis and Exodus and also cites passages
from elsewhere in the Bible (though it is not clear that his
'canon' included any books beyond the Pentateuch).

Emphasis on the text seems to have developed especially in
the Diaspora where most Jews did not have ready access to the
temple. Since the focus of worship had been and remained
the temple and its cult until it was destroyed in 70 CE, it was
a central symbol to most Jews, whether or not they lived near
Jerusalem. Yet the lack of opportunity to worship at the temple
by large numbers of Jews living outside Palestine meant the
need for some other religious centre in their daily lives. This led
first to a concentration on sacred writings and then to a community institution where these religious writings could be read
and studied: the synagogue. The synagogue is first attested in
the Diaspora about the middle of the third century BCE, during
the early Greek period. It was also about this time that the
Pentateuch was translated into Greek, suggesting a need for the
Greek-speaking community to have the scriptures in their own
vernacular. Judaism as a 'religion of the book', and the synagogue as the focus of the community, seem to have developed
first in the Diaspora and were only imported into Palestine from
there.

Some Jewish groups evidently regarded the Jerusalem temple
as polluted, which meant that they kept it at arm's length.

Sacred writings thus assumed considerable importance to them. The Essenes studied sacred scripture in whatever form it took with them. If the Qumran commentaries are Essene in origin, it is here that we have the most detailed biblical exegesis of a pre-70 Jewish sect. But even those groups accepting the temple were also interested in the written word by the time of the later Greek and Roman periods. According to Josephus and the New Testament, the Sadducees claimed to confine themselves to the written text, though we must assume that they developed their own tradition of interpretation – scripture does not automatically interpret itself. The Pharisees are alleged to have had traditions not found in the written text. To what extent this tradition was based on exegesis and to what extent it was really parabiblical (that is, separate from the biblical tradition but parallel to it) is a matter of debate, especially since it is not clear that any Pharisaic traditions have survived (apart from a few brief ones in the New Testament and possibly in Josephus). However, if many of these traditions were taken up into rabbinic literature (albeit in revised, edited, and recontextualized form), as often argued, then some of them seem to be closely connected with the text of the Pentateuch while others appear to be quite different and independent.

The general outlook of the Sadducees, Pharisees, and Essenes on revolution and opposition to foreign rule may have varied and taken different forms. Nevertheless, all three groups were involved at some time or other in attempts to rid the country of foreign domination. Along with blatantly revolutionary groups such as the Sicarii and the Zealots, important Pharisees and Essenes are identified as taking part in the 66–70 revolt against Rome, and we can infer that Sadducees were also among the rebels. It has been asserted that the Pharisees and the Essenes did not actively fight against Roman rule. We do not know enough to be sure whether there was a 'group policy' on the question, but we know of specific individuals from those groups who were high up in the revolutionary council. Simon ben Gamaliel, the son of Gamaliel I (apparently the same as Gamaliel the Pharisee mentioned in Acts 5), was a part of the Jerusalem leadership in the early part of the war. As the revolt got underway, the 'notable Pharisees' were part of discussions of how to react to those pushing the country into war. Similarly, John the Essene was a leader killed early in the war. There are also some indications that members of the Qumran community were among the defenders at Masada. Assuming this is so, and assuming Qumran was Essene (both substantial assumptions), the Essenes as a whole were willing to fight under certain conditions.

At this distance from the events, it is difficult to distinguish what was political and what was religious in the various revolutionary movements. Indeed, they may have been so conjoined that they could not be separated. In any case, it seems clear that religious ideology lies behind some of the revolutionary movements, if not all. The 'Fourth Philosophy' (of which the Sicarii are possibly the heirs) is said to have opposed Roman rule on specifically religious grounds: only God should be the ruler of the Jewish people (3.5). We also know of one group waiting for divine deliverance even as the Romans were breaking through into the temple itself in the last day of the war (3.6). Other groups seem to have some sort of ideology behind them simply because of their behaviour, even when the historical sources are hostile and present them only as common bandits. High ideals can of course be used as a cloak for base motives and actions, so we must be careful not to read religious motives into every riot and example of agitation. What can be said is that many of the opposition movements claimed – whether sincerely or not – to be serving God, and the revolts they instituted an example of laying their lives down as an act of worship.

Opposition to foreign rule did not have to take the form of violent action or outright rebellion. There were those who believed that 'they also serve who only stand and wait'. In many apocalyptic and related writings, the emphasis is not on what men do but what God does. They describe a history which is more or less foreordained. Israel may do certain things, and the Gentiles may do certain things, but none of their actions ultimately affect the divine plan. Exactly how that plan unfolded varied from writer to writer. For many, all history would be leading to a period of troubles and even cosmic cataclysm that would immediately precede the intervention of God and the creation of 'new heavens and a new earth'. Others saw a more gradual and less tumultuous ushering in of God's kingdom, without the cosmic upheaval found in many apocalypses. But in all these scenarios, it is God who takes the action, not the people. In a book such as Daniel (11:33–35) and the *Testament of Moses* (9), the righteous do their bit by giving themselves up to martyrdom, but they do not take up arms against the oppressor.

In various writings, both apocalyptic and otherwise, a messianic figure or figures appear(s). In some cases, this is a warrior figure who will destroy the enemies of Israel, with God's help, and bring the nations into subjection to Israel and the true God. This sort of messianic figure seems to be modelled on the Old Testament passages which talk of a king like David whom God will raise up to bring an idealized state to Israel (Jeremiah 33:14–22). Yet it must be recognized that there was no single 'Messiah' or 'messianic expectation' among the Jews of this time; on the contrary, the concept and also the importance of the Messiah seems to have varied considerably. Some texts envisage a heavenly figure who comes to earth. Some Qumran texts mention two messianic figures, one from Israel and another from Aaron (a 'secular' and a priestly Messiah). There were also circles for whom the idea was completely absent, judging from the texts which give no hint of the concept (even when it might have been expected if it was important to the writer).

Like the more particular 'messianic expectations', eschatological views in general were also diverse in conception and significance. Eschatology covers a range of sub-topics, including endtime events, life after death, and indeed Messianism itself. What stands out is the wide range of views on the subject, seemingly extending from one extreme to another. On the question of life after death, much of the Hebrew Bible seems not to have had such an idea. Death brought the end of the person as such, though there was something which survived in Sheol in a shadowy way. This was also the position of Ben Sira about 200 BCE. To the best of our knowledge, this seems to have been the position of the Sadducees, as well, though our sources are rather vague.

Some texts envisage a resurrection, but even this takes more than one form. Some think of a restoration of the original physical person to life, but others clearly think of a 'resurrection of the spirit'. Widespread in Jewish texts is the concept of the immortality of the soul which leaves the body at death and is rewarded or punished. This belief in the soul may or may not be combined with the idea of a resurrection and final judgement.

Therefore, the question of what happens at the endtime varies from text to text. Indeed, some texts seem to think of an endtime only in the sense of the death and post-mortem reward or punishment of the individual but do not suggest any cosmic eschatology. But in many of the texts which expect the end of the present age and a new, changed age to come, there are attempts to calculate when that end will come. Some of these sources divide history up into discreet periods, though these are not usually sufficiently specific to allow the exact calculation of when the end will come. Some texts discuss the age of the world, however, and explicitly or implicitly suggest that the world will last for only a certain specific period of time. Therefore, if one can know how old the world is now and how long its total age is supposed to be, the time remaining can be worked out. Other texts give other sorts of figures, such as the 70 years of Jeremiah and its reinterpretation as the 70 weeks of years in Daniel. Assuming that the world would come to an end, there was an understandable desire to know how long before that happened. Many texts, such as those from Qumran, assume that the readers are living at the end of the age.

The pluralistic nature of Judaism is exemplified by considering elements of it which some may find incompatible with their views on 'orthodoxy'. This includes elements like magic and the other esoteric arts (astrology, divination, exorcism, healing), 'miracle-working', and Gnosticism. It is not easy to get at the place of these elements in Judaism because of the nature of the sources; this makes discussion of them speculative to some extent. Nevertheless, there is enough evidence preserved to suggest that these were important constituents of the mosaic we call pre-70 Judaism. The Gnostic texts, though much later than 70 in their present form, still have many early Jewish traditions in them – traditions which are not just borrowed from the Hebrew Bible but represent Jewish interpretations of the OT text. The source of these traditions seems to be Judaism itself, yet the Gnostic texts in their present form are generally hostile to Judaism. This suggests a portion of Judaism which reinterpreted the Old Testament and Jewish traditions in such a way that it finally led – no doubt, through various stages – to a world view which was anti-Jewish. Those who argue that at least a portion of Gnosticism grew out of Judaism seem to have the weight of the argument on their side, though how and when is more difficult to answer.

I have been focusing on streams to illustrate the diversity of Second Temple Judaism. But it should not be assumed that these were completely independent streams: as already noted, they might run parallel or even merge, as well as flow contrary to one another. For example, there are good arguments that a strong priestly input went into apocalypticism. Members of all three of the main sects contributed to revolution at some point. In some areas of religion, there was a good deal of common belief and thought among the various Jewish groups; in others, much diversity. In the matter of worship, the centrality of the temple cult meant a good deal of shared practice. Although the current priesthood might be criticized, even severely, by some groups (such as Qumran), it is difficult to find more than one or two examples of people who rejected the Jerusalem temple outright.

This is why the destruction of the temple in 70 was such a crucial event. The trauma is well illustrated in such writings as 4 Ezra and 2 Baruch. The pre-70 Jewish groups which survived were those who carried within their religious system the means to transcend the loss of the temple. The apocalypticists, the temple-based groups, and various others disappeared after 70, not always straight away but with time. The Christians had Christ and did not need a temple. They survived and eventually flourished, first as a stream within Judaism but ultimately becoming a separate religion. Rabbinic Judaism was a post-70 development. It probably contained a synthesis of several pre-70 elements, but the one factor which allowed it to survive was making study of the Torah central to its religious practice. This replaced the temple. A functioning cult was no longer necessary, though discussion and debate about it formed a prime subject of study. Study was an act of worship. Study had taken the place of the sacrificial cult. Any religious movement develops diversity, and rabbinic Judaism was no exception. It also took time – centuries – for the rabbis to establish their authority and impose their views on the Jewish community.

Rabbinic Judaism developed its own currents and variety. Yet the new situation seemed in many ways much more monolithic when compared to the enormous variety and plurality of forms existing in the Second Temple period. Too often the stereotyped image of 'orthodox' Judaism or Christianity has been used to construct Judaism before 70. The many different currents becoming apparent in recent scholarly study belies that model. This book has drawn attention in a brief way to the variety of differences and the pluralism of pre-70 Judaism. Study in greater depth confirms this diversity. The complexity of the religious phenomenon we call Second Temple Judaism forces itself more and more upon us, the more we study it.

CITATION INDEX

Bible and Early Christian Writings

INDEX OF NAMES AND SUBJECTS

INDEX OF MODERN NAMES